Disclaimer

This book intended to provide our readers with information and motivation. It is a sold with the knowledge that the publisher is not engaged to provide any form of psychological, legal, or other professional advice. Each page's content is the sold expression and opinion of the author. Neither the publisher not the individual author (s) shall be responsible for any physical, psychological, emotional, financial, or commercial damages, including but not limited to special, incidental, consequential, or other damages. Our point of view and rights are the same: you are solely accountable for your decisions, actions, and outcomes.

- Disclaimer 3
- 1. Introduction: The Search for Eternal Wealth 6
- 2. Chapter 1: The Basis of Good Luck 8
  - 2.1: The Start Small Principle 12
  - 2.2: Savings Habits: The Foundation for Wealth 16
  - 2.3: Financial Guidance from Babylon's Streets 21
- 3. Chapter 2: The Prosperity Golden Rules 25
  - 3.1: The Five Golden Rules 30
  - 3.2: The Art of Making Money Work for You 34
  - 3.3: The Value of Sensible Investing 42
- 4. Chapter 3: The Secret of the Lender 48
  - 4.1: Safe Lending Strategy 52
  - 4.2: Evaluation of Risk and Benefit 57
  - 4.3: Compound Interest's Power 61
- 5. Chapter 4: The Mentality of the Merchant 65
  - 5.1: The Ethic of Marketing 69
  - 5.2: Adding Worth to Assets 73
  - 5.3: The Success Code for Merchants 77
- 6. Chapter 5: The Wealth Guardian 82
  - 6.1: Safeguarding Your Resources 86
  - 6.2: Insurance's Place in Preserving Wealth 90
  - 6.3: Legacy Building and Estate Planning 95
- 7. Chapter 6: The Road to Plenty 100
  - 7.1: The Path to Personal Development 105
  - 7.3: Wealth Is Not Just Financial 113
- 8. Conclusion: Babylon's Richest Man of Today 117

Wealth's Ancient Secrets

Unveiling The Richest Man in Babylon

By

William M. Upshaw

Copyright © 2024 William M. Upshaw

All rights reserved. No part of this book may be reproduced transmitted in any form or by any means, electronic, or mechanical, including photocopying, recording, or by any information storage and retrieval system, without written permission from the author, accept by a reviewer who may summarize brief passages in a review.

9. Appendix: Financial Growth Instruments and Resources..121

1. Introduction: The Search for Eternal Wealth

Beneath the opulent ziggurats and bustling marketplaces of ancient Babylon, there once flourished a secret so deep that it has reverberated through the ages, whispering to all who choose to listen the true meaning of wealth. Kings and commoners alike have searched after this knowledge, which was once known only to the richest man in Babylon, yet it has remained elusive to many. It is the pursuit of eternal wealth, a voyage that goes beyond the amassing of gold and silver to the core of success.

Together, let's weave the historical tapestries to reveal the long-forgotten mysteries that have influenced the course of empires and individual lives across the millennia. The book "Wealth's Ancient Secrets: Unveiling the Richest Man in Babylon" is more than just a book; it's a treasure map that opens doors to timeless wealth and knowledge. It is an invitation to adventure for those with the guts to go in search of wealth that is not attainable with paper money.

The pursuit of timeless prosperity involves both an internal and an exterior shift. It's a route paved with timeless values, values that have been recorded on clay tablets for future generations and murmured in the breezes of Babylon. These ideas apply to managing life in general, not simply managing finances. They teach us that genuine wealth is shared rather than hoarded, acknowledged rather than bragged about, and prudently grown rather than carelessly wasted.

You will learn the secrets of fortune that allowed Babylon's richest man to accumulate money that outlasted him in the pages that follow. You'll discover the universal principles of prosperity that have enabled people to realize their aspirations. You will study the thinking of the merchant, the lender's trade secret, and the guardian's function in preserving and increasing wealth. Finally, you will set out on the path of abundance, where the accumulation of wealth and the pursuit of personal development converge to unveil treasures that transcend temporal boundaries.

You will discover when you explore the ancient wisdom in this book that the keys to prosperity are not buried in forgotten tombs or tucked away in enigmatic writings. They are there in the parables that have been handed down through the ages, the stories of people who have traversed the streets of Babylon, and the very fabric of nature itself.

Seeking everlasting prosperity is an honorable endeavor requiring bravery, self-control, and an unwavering curiosity. It's an endeavor that pushes us to search for prosperity that endures rather than being seduced by the flashy glamour of worldly belongings. It's an endeavor that asks us to take control of our own lives and leave a legacy that encourages others to start their search for everlasting prosperity.

With the promise of wealth as our destination and the wisdom of the ancients serving as our guide, let's embark on this epic trip together. Let the search for everlasting wealth commence.

2. Chapter 1: The Basis of Good Luck

The city of Babylon is remembered in history as a symbol of human inventiveness and the unwavering quest for prosperity. Here, in the middle of the fertile crescent, civilization first discovered how to maximize the resources of the environment and the potential of its people. The principles of fortune, established in Babylon, have stood the test of time and continue to teach us valuable lessons about accumulating wealth and achieving financial prosperity.

The tale of Babylon is not only one of wealth; it is also one of tenacity, inventiveness, and strategic foresight. It is a history that starts with the most fundamental yet deep realization of wealth: that it is a tool, not a goal, for creating a thriving community and a happy existence.

The True Nature of Wealth

One must first comprehend the nature of money in order to learn the foundations of fortune. The sheer amassing of possessions or the stashing of gold coins in secret vaults do not constitute wealth. It is the capacity to add value, make better use of resources, and promote prosperity and personal development for both the individual and the community.

In Babylon, the weight of one's purse and the impact of one's contributions dictated one's degree of prosperity. The richest people were those who created trade routes to far-off places, constructed aqueducts to irrigate farms, and drafted legislation to defend the rights of both merchants and citizens.

The Trust Currency

The currency of confidence was vital to the economy of Babylon. Transactions included promises of honor in addition to the exchange of goods. More than just legal records, the clay tablets that kept track of obligations and agreements were also symbols of confidence between the people they belonged to and the community they supported.

This trust served as the foundation for the economy's success. It made possible the investments, credit extensions, and financial flows that supported growth and innovation. The wealth of Babylon would evaporate like dust in the breeze of the desert, and the foundations of fortune would collapse in the absence of trust.

The Expansion of Available Resources

Multiplying resources was the foundation of Babylon's success. The city's surrounding lush fields were carefully farmed, transforming the desolate plains into abundant harvests. The Euphrates River flowed through the town and was used for transportation, food, and water supply.

However, resource multiplication extended beyond trade and agriculture. It encompassed the human spirit as well as the artisans and craftspeople who, through guilds and apprenticeships, increased their knowledge and skill sets. It was demonstrated by the scribes and intellectuals who wrote wisdom down on clay tablets for posterity, so multiplying its value.

The Spread of Income

The people of Babylon understood that they needed to spread their riches in order to maintain it. They made investments in a range of industries, including farming, metallurgy, textiles, and trade. This diversification protected against war, starvation, and recessions.

The development of diverse skill sets and the search for multiple revenue streams were other aspects of diversification. It was recognized that depending only on one source of income was as unstable as erecting a house on the sand.

The Art of Saving

The discipline of saving is one of Babylon's most enduring lessons. The richest man in Babylon, whose secrets we will try to solve, understood that careful saving was necessary to accumulate long-term wealth. A percentage of every profit was saved to be used as the seed for future expansion rather than to be handled or wasted.

The handling of expenses was also subject to this regulation. The Babylonians were very careful to discern needs from wants and to make investments that would increase their riches rather than spend them.

Investment Wisdom

Without financial wisdom, fortune's foundations are not complete. The Babylonians were shrewd investors who were constantly looking for chances to make money. They were aware of the hazards and sought advice from experts before parting with their hard-earned cash.

In addition to enterprises and real estate, investments were made in youth education and public health. Investing in people was just as important to the Babylonians as investing in material possessions.

The Heritage of Affluence

Lastly, the legacy of money is included in the foundations of fortune. The richest man in Babylon did not think of riches as a personal badge to be kept close to the vest. Rather, he viewed it as a legacy to be left behind, a way to empower the next generations and advance society.

This legacy extended beyond gold and silver to include the timeless ideas that governed the accumulation and administration of riches. It was a legacy of morality, ethics, and an overarching vision that went beyond any one person.

Let us keep in mind that the ideas that survive, rather than just the glittering money, are the foundations of fortune as we delve deeper into the secrets of the richest man in Babylon. These eternal riches concepts, which hold today just as they did in ancient Babylon, are what will direct us on our journey.

2.1: The Start Small Principle

One very important but frequently disregarded rule in the chase of money is to start small. This idea is the foundation of progress and prosperity; it is not just a tactic. It is a philosophy. The greatest visionaries and business people—including the richest man in Babylon himself—have accepted this idea. Starting small is like sowing the seeds of prosperity in the rich soil of endurance and nourishing them with the waters of hard work until they blossom into the majestic, tall trees of plenty.

The Lowly Origins

Every major undertaking starts with a single step, a small deed that initiates the course of history. The wealthiest individual in Babylon recognized that the most elaborate mansions were constructed meticulously, with each brick placed one after the other. He was aware that the most powerful empires originated from little city-states, building their foundations one shovelful of dirt at a time deep into the ground.

It's important to embrace the modest beginnings and understand that the first step is where a thousand miles begin when you start small. It's about realizing that even the world's most intricate systems started as straightforward concepts that were fostered and evolved.

Compound Growth's Power

The power of compound growth is inextricably related to the idea of starting small. Through the power of compounding, a tiny investment can expand dramatically, just like a single grain of sand can tilt the scales. Compound growth has a straightforward yet profound formula:

A is equal to P \left (1 + \frac{r}{n} \right) ^{nt}.

Where:

- After (n) years, the total amount of money accumulated, including interest, is (A).

- The main amount (the starting sum of money) is denoted by (P).

The yearly interest rate is denoted as (r) in decimal.

The number of times interest is compounded annually is (n).

- (t) is the number of years that the money is invested.

This formula is the motor for wealth creation; it is the rhythm that drives the growth of small investments into gigantic fortunes. When given enough time and patience, it is the quiet power that can multiply a small amount into a king's ransom.

The Incremental Progress Discipline

Initiating modestly also represents the discipline of gradual advancement. It is the routine of consistently making tiny, gradual advancements that add up over time. The person pursuing money must chip away at their objectives, day by day, with unshakable focus and commitment, much as the sculptor chips away at the marble block with thousands of exact knocks.

Patience is required for this discipline because results might not show up right away. However, it is precisely this same patience that distinguishes the fleeting from the permanent, the flicker of a pan from the radiance of an everlasting flame.

The Risk Mitigation Strategy

The risk-reduction plan is among the strongest arguments in favor of starting small. Smaller stakes initially allow one to experiment, learn from the experience, and make changes without worrying about suffering a disastrous loss. The wealthiest man in Babylon divided his risks, investing a small amount of money in a number of different ventures and learning and developing from each one rather than risking all on one big bet.

This method enables the growth of competence and the acquisition of knowledge. It acts as a safety net, making sure that failure in one endeavor does not equal disaster. This approach recognizes that every step—no matter how small—is a crucial lesson in the art of creating wealth and values the trip just as much as the destination.

The Quality of Modesty

Humility exercises also involve starting small. It serves as a reminder that one's goals, no matter how lofty, must be based on reality. It teaches that conceit is the antithesis of progress and that genuine development arises from a position of humility and deference to the method.

The richest guy in Babylon did not show off his possessions or his achievements. Rather, he conducted his business in silence, beginning small, expanding gradually, and imparting his knowledge to those who wished to learn it. His strength was his humility, and it was this quality that enabled him to create a legacy that would last for all time.

The Self-Discovery Journey

Ultimately, self-discovery is a journey that begins small. One discovers their passions and worries, as well as their skills and shortcomings, by taking tiny steps. True self-awareness is found in the silent times of introspection when one evaluates the advancement made from modest beginnings.

This quest is about more than just gaining wealth; it's about realizing one's place in the world and discovering meaning and purpose in the chase of success. It's a path that challenges not only one's capacity for acquisition but also one's capacity for personal growth.

To sum up, the foundation of building riches is the idea of starting small. It is a notion that instills humility, self-control, and patience. It's a theory that reduces danger and encourages introspection. When accepted, this idea has the potential to grow into enormous, prosperous trees that are firmly anchored in good fortune.

2.2: Savings Habits: The Foundation for Wealth

The road to riches is like climbing a very tall mountain. It takes planning, stamina, and a sequence of systematic, steady steps. The first and most important of these actions is the habit of saving. It is the base upon which the structure of financial stability is constructed and the seed that gives rise to the tree of wealth. With careful cultivation, this habit can turn even the lowest incomes into a sizeable fortune.

The Savings Philosophy

Savings is a philosophy that represents a cautious and forward-thinking way of thinking, not just a specific behavior. It is the understanding that Making plans is not only a decision but also a requirement. And that it will hold equal significance to the present. The wealthiest man in Babylon did not get rich by accident or inheritance; rather, he became wealthy by embracing a saving philosophy that looked beyond the present moment's satisfactions to the possibilities of the future.

This way of thinking stems from the knowledge that life is erratic and that luck can swing with the same quickness as the sands in a desert shift with the wind. By saving, one constructs a defense against the unanticipated and a stronghold against the vagaries of fate.

The Art of Saving

Saving is a discipline that needs to be consistently exercised. Saving money on occasion or when circumstances allow is insufficient; one needs to make saving money a regular component of their financial routine. The wealthiest man in Babylon advocated paying oneself first, putting aside at least 10 percent of one's income before covering other bills.

Living within one's means, ignoring the allure of needless spending, and putting long-term financial stability ahead of momentary pleasures are all examples of this discipline. It's a discipline that calls for self-control and a distinct understanding of one's economic objectives.

The Way Savings Work

There are basic mechanics involved in the act of saving. The first step is to create a budget, which is a comprehensive plan that divides up the money into several categories for requirements and wants while making sure some is saved. Realistic spending must be included in this budget, taking into account one's income, expenses, and financial goals.

The next step after creating the budget is opening a savings account, ideally with interest. It is best to keep this account distinct from one's checking account in order to lessen the temptation to withdraw funds for regular needs. Even more process simplification can be achieved via automatic transfers, which guarantee that savings are set aside without requiring manual intervention.

Compound Interest's Power

The power of compound interest is among the strongest arguments for making saving a habit. Albert Einstein often refers to compound interest as the eighth wonder of the world and with good reason. The following is the compound interest formula:

$$A = P\left(1 + \frac{r}{n}\right)^{nt}$$

Where:

- After (n) years, the total amount of money accumulated, including interest, is (A).
- The initial sum of money, or the main amount, is shown by (P).

The yearly interest rate is denoted as (r) in decimal.

The number of times interest is compounded annually is (n).

- (t) is the number of years that the money is invested.

Compound interest allows even modest savings over time to accumulate into substantial quantities. It proves the proverb "time is money" and offers the patient saver a windfall that greatly outweighs their initial outlay.

The Psychological Advantages of Preservation

There are psychological advantages to saving as well. Knowing that one is ready for crises or unanticipated chances gives one peace of mind. It gives one a sense of success and gives them power over their financial future. Observing the growth of one's money may be a very fulfilling experience that strengthens the habit and motivates additional savings.

Furthermore, saving money can encourage more deliberate spending. It motivates people to assess the real worth of their goods and make better financial decisions. By enabling a more purposeful and intentional manner of living, this mindfulness can be applied to various aspects of life.

The Effects of Saving on Society

Additionally, saving has a wider social influence. By lowering reliance on credit and lowering susceptibility to downturns in the economy, it promotes economic stability. It can result in more money being spent on community projects, businesses, and education, which will encourage development and innovation.

Saving money can help people personally sustain their families, give to charitable organizations, and leave a legacy for future generations. It's a practice that benefits the saver personally and has the potential to improve society at large.

The Difficulties of Conserving

Saving money has numerous advantages, but it also has drawbacks. The discipline of saving can be challenging to uphold in a society that frequently places a higher value on consuming and getting what you want right away. It necessitates swimming against the flow of consumerism and enduring the relentless onslaught of advertising messages that promote consumption.

A lot of people may find saving difficult due to economic variables, including inflation, low salaries, and expensive living expenses. To develop methods to save in the face of these obstacles, one must be resourceful, creative, and occasionally willing to make sacrifices.

The Road to Financial Success

In the end, the first step toward prosperity is developing the habit of saving. It serves as the cornerstone for prosperity and financial stability. Once formed, it's a habit that can trigger a series of prudent financial practices, such as retirement planning and smart investing.

Let's not forget that modest, regular acts are what start the journey rather than huge gestures as we continue to delve into the age-old mysteries of prosperity. Despite its apparent simplicity, the practice of saving has a significant influence. It is the first step toward prosperity and the key that opens the door to an abundant future.

2.3: Financial Guidance from Babylon's Streets

Babylon's streets were more than just commercial avenues; they served as vital conduits for the dissemination of antiquated knowledge. It was in these shadowy alleys and bustling marketplaces that the common people of Babylon acquired and disseminated the financial expertise that would ensure their prosperity. Even though it is old, this wisdom contains timeless truths that can help anyone navigate contemporary streets in pursuit of financial enlightenment.

Using the Market as a School

In Babylon, the marketplace served as both a venue for trade and a living classroom where every day economic concepts were taught. The trade of things, the wrangling over costs, and the skill of negotiating taught us about human psychology, value judgment, and supply and demand.

Through their triumphs and setbacks, traders and merchants imparted knowledge on the value of comprehending one's market, knowing when to give in and when to hold strong on a price. They demonstrated that everyone ready to watch and study could acquire financial wisdom, which was not just found in palaces and temples.

The Prosperity Parables

The parables and fables that captured the financial knowledge of the ages resounded through the streets of Babylon. These oral traditions, handed down from one generation to the next, were more than just amusement; they were also means of knowledge, with the secrets of prosperity included within their stories.

According to one such story, a poor guy saved one copper penny every day until he had enough money to purchase a clay pot. By carrying water for the wealthy with this pot, he was able to earn additional cash, which he saved up to buy more pots. He gradually established a company that supported his family and created jobs for others, demonstrating the value of investing and saving money.

The Strategy Scrolls of the Scribes

The scribes of Babylon documented the financial transactions, yet their scrolls held information beyond just figures. They carried financial management techniques, success stories from past endeavors, and cautionary tales about disastrous choices.

These scrolls were a veritable gold mine of information, emphasizing the need for meticulous record-keeping for prosperity. They demonstrated that maintaining a record of earnings and outlays, keeping an eye on investments, and making plans were just as important as actually making money.

Lessons from Lenders

The lenders of Babylon were risk and reward instructors as much as creditors. They gave an example of the value of conducting due diligence and evaluating a borrower's moral fiber and ability to repay. They demonstrated how lending might lead to prosperity, but only if done carefully and wisely.

In order to guarantee that loans were secured against assets that could be reclaimed in the case of default, the lenders also imparted knowledge on the importance of collateral. They were able to lend with confidence since this practice safeguarded their riches and served as a safety net.

The Art of Asset Building by the Artisans

With their deft hands and inventive brains, the artisans of Babylon were masters at creating assets. They realized that their biggest advantage was their talent and that by perfecting their craft, they could produce valuable goods that would fetch a higher price in the market.

These craftsmen imparted the knowledge that developing one's abilities was just as vital as purchasing gold or real estate. They demonstrated how gaining knowledge and making constant improvements may raise one's value and, in turn, one's riches.

The Growth Principles for Gardeners

The Babylonian gardeners personified the concepts of growth that pertained to prosperity as they tended their plots of land. They understood that just as wealth requires time, attention, and ideal circumstances to thrive, so too did gardens demand time, care, and the correct conditions.

They propagated the idea that planting a range of crops would help to diversify and guard against the failure of any one harvest. They demonstrated how routine upkeep, such as weeding and planting, was comparable to budgeting and caring for investments.

The Equity Ethos of the Elders

Respected for their knowledge and experience, Babylon's elders preserved the values of justice and equity. They advised that money should always be acquired honestly, that ethical behavior should always be upheld in economic relations, and that pursuing financial gain should never come at the expense of morality.

Their knowledge served as a reminder to the populace that material possessions did not just determine genuine riches but also the respect and confidence one earned via right and moral behavior.

Babylonian Wisdom's Legacy

Through the decades, the financial knowledge gleaned from the streets of Babylon has persisted. It is a corpus of knowledge that offers insights that are just as applicable today as they were thousands of years ago, transcending both time and culture.

Let us take the lessons learned from the streets of Babylon with us as we stroll through our towns. Let us study, absorb, and put into practice the age-old knowledge that has led innumerable spirits to wealth and financial stability. Remember that the secrets of wealth are not hidden in closed volumes or exclusive circles; instead, they are waiting to be discovered through everyday interactions in life.

In conclusion, the financial sagacity of the Babylonian streets bears witness to the durability of good economic ideas. It's a wisdom that instructs us to pay attention, absorb, and apply historical lessons to the present and future. When accepted, this wisdom can take us all the way to the base of luck and beyond.

3. Chapter 2: The Prosperity Golden Rules

Throughout history, people have been continuously striving for prosperity, leading societies to look for the golden principles governing affluence. These timeless, wise guidelines are not just suggestions; rather, they are fundamental ideas that have been shown to foster prosperity and success. These ideas were not just recognized but also practiced in the ancient city of Babylon, producing some of the richest people and a long-lasting culture.

The Visionary Goal-Setting Rule

Setting definite, ambitious goals is the first golden rule of prosperity. Wealth originates from the vision of one's goals in the mind. The Babylonians saw that the road to wealth turned into an aimless, meandering path in the absence of a defined destination. They established aspirational but attainable goals that acted as compass points for their choices and activities.

These goals weren't just idle aspirations; plans and strategies outlining the steps necessary to realize the vision were in place to support them. They included not only their wealth but also the well-being of their families, companies, and local communities.

The Consistent Effort Rule

The dedication to consistent work is the second golden guideline. The Babylonians understood that wealth came from constant, hard work rather than as a gift from the gods. They held in high regard the values of diligence and tenacity because they knew that these traits were what propelled advancement.

This rule highlights the fact that success is the result of consistent everyday work that builds up over time rather than an overnight event. A plentiful harvest is the product of constant fieldwork, while wealth and mastery are the outcomes of the unrelenting pursuit of perfection.

The Financial Education Rule

The quest for financial education represents the third golden guideline. The Babylonians made significant investments in their financial literacy since knowledge is a valuable asset that never loses value. They aimed to comprehend the laws of wealth accumulation, the complexities of trade, and the fundamentals of economics.

With the help of financial education, they were able to identify possibilities, make well-informed decisions, and stay away from mistakes that could have cost them everything. It was a lifetime endeavor that started in the scribes' schools and carried on through the marketplace exchanges.

The Prudent Investment Rule

The sensible investment practice is the fourth golden guideline. The Babylonians were methodical investors rather than careless gamblers. They were aware of the significance of risk assessment, portfolio diversification, and making investments in businesses that offered a respectable rate of return.

They made investments in their city's infrastructure, companies, youth education, and land. These investments served as the foundation for the enormous oaks of their riches, which have supported and fed successive generations.

The Generosity Rule

The practice of giving is the fifth golden rule. The Babylonians believed that prosperity should be shared rather than hoarded. They were proponents of the sharing of riches and the importance of giving back to the society that helped them in their pursuits.

Giving was viewed as an investment in society that would pay off in the form of a flourishing, stable neighborhood. It was also an indication of character, proof that real wealth was measured in goodwill rather than just gold.

The Adaptability Rule

Embracing flexibility is the sixth golden guideline. The Babylonians prospered because they were adaptable and sensitive to the shifting conditions in their surroundings since they lived in a world that was always changing. They were open to changing their tactics and methods in order to take advantage of fresh chances and meet new problems. They were not set in their ways.

Their ability to adapt meant that they continued to be at the forefront of invention, that their strategies for generating riches changed as the times did, and that their prosperity persisted even during times of change and turmoil.

The Ethical Conduct Rule

Following moral principles is the seventh golden rule. The prosperity based on deception or exploitation was a house constructed on sand that would eventually fall, as the Babylonians understood. They behaved honorably in their economic activities, keeping their word and showing consideration for others.

Behaving morally promoted trust, which is a resource just as important as any precious gold. Establishing relationships and opening avenues that aided in their wealth made sure that their reputation came before them.

The Legacy Building Rule

The emphasis on legacy building is the eighth golden rule. The Babylonians saw riches as a legacy to be built and maintained for future generations rather than as a transient objective. They took steps to ensure that their fortunes would benefit not only themselves but also those who came after them, as well as to safeguard their wealth and educate their heirs.

The goal of legacy building was to leave a lasting impression on others, serve as a reference point for others to establish their prosperity, and be a tribute to the individual's life's work.

The Equilibrium Rule

Keeping things in balance is the ninth golden rule. The Babylonians realized that having money was not the only factor in leading a happy life. They tried to strike a balance between their quest for wealth and their spiritual, relational, and physical well-being.

In order to ensure that their pursuit of prosperity did not come at the expense of their happiness or the welfare of their society, balance prevented the excesses that could result in disaster.

The Gratitude Rule

The development of thankfulness is the eleventh golden rule. The Babylonians acknowledged their wealth as a blessing that needed to be appreciated and stewarded, and they were thankful for it. Having gratitude helped them stay grounded by serving as a constant reminder of their low beginnings and the teamwork that made them successful.

Their feeling of gratitude closed the circle of success by ensuring that everyone appreciated and enjoyed the money they had accumulated.

To sum up, the golden rules of prosperity are timeless ideas that lead to prosperity and abundance for both people and civilizations. These are guidelines that, when diligently and wisely followed, can result in a prosperous life that is rich in more than just worldly possessions. They are Babylon's heritage, a past gift to the future, and a path to prosperity for those who choose to follow them.

3.1: The Five Golden Rules

Wealth in the ancient city of Babylon was frequently the consequence of upholding a set of enduring ideals rather than being the product of luck or inheritance. Of these, the Five Laws of Gold are particularly noteworthy as essential principles that helped both the wealthy and the aspirant to financial success. These laws offer a guide for acquiring and safeguarding riches, and they are just as applicable now as they were back when chariots and clay tablets were common.

The First Law: Those Who Save Shall Receive Gold Gladly

The first law, which states that you should save at least 10% of your income, is fundamental to sound money management. The foundation for anyone looking to accumulate riches is this law. Your savings account will determine your fortune, not the amount of gold you acquire. Saving money is a discipline that distinguishes the sensible from the foolish, as well as a statement of will and dedication to the future.

The cornerstone of wealth creation is saving. It serves as a reserve for seizing chances and enduring crises. The Babylonians were aware that individuals who saved chose a route where wealth was happily received because of their self-control and foresight.

The Second Law: Gold Works Hard for the Savvy Owner Who Finds Useful Jobs for It

The second law emphasizes the significance of using your gold to benefit you. Savings alone are insufficient; prudent investment is also required. You have to do something with the gold you save, like make some more money. This law encompasses the notion of passive income or the hope that your money will increase without your active labor.

Carefully selecting investments is necessary, keeping security and return in mind. The Babylonians realized that gold could support its owner long after they retired from the workforce if it was invested sensibly and became a steady stream of income.

The Third Law states that gold clings to the cautious owner's protection when they invest it based on the counsel of wise men.

When investing in gold, the third law advises using wisdom and caution. It cautions against impatience and the lure of instant wealth, which can result in rash choices and financial ruin. The Babylonians respected the counsel of experts in managing gold because they knew that such knowledge might safeguard their riches.

This law instructs people to seek out experienced consultants who have a track record of building and safeguarding wealth. It serves as a reminder that everyone may gain from the knowledge and experience of others, even the most intelligent.

According to the Fourth Law, money invested in endeavors or objectives that are foreign to the investor or that have not received approval from qualified managers tends to elude them.

The fourth law serves as a cautionary tale about the perils of unfamiliarity and ignorance. Wealth, according to this saying, will evade those who invest in ventures they don't fully understand or haven't had in-depth analysis from professionals. The Babylonians understood that information was power, especially when it came to making investments.

This law emphasizes how crucial it is to know where your money is going and to make sure that industry professionals approve the investment. It is an appeal to become knowledgeable, comprehend the nuances of one's investments, and stay away from the traps of ignorance.

The Fifth Law states that gold runs away from those who would force it to achieve impossible profits, heed the seductive advice of con artists and scammers, or rely solely on their romantic investment desires and inexperience.

The fifth law serves as a warning against falling for people who promise unrealistic earnings and their enticing methods. It serves as a sobering reminder that even the most passionate chaser of gold will fail if they seek it with irrational expectations. The Babylonians were aware that extravagant returns were frequently used as a cover for dishonesty and disappointment.

This law advises that investments should be sound and grounded in realistic expectations, and that one should temper their wishes with reality. It advocates for moderate and consistent progress, cautioning against the temptation to pursue rapid prosperity.

In summary, the Five Laws of Gold are primarily about attitude as much as behavior. They impart discipline, wisdom, caution, knowledge, and realism to investors and savers. These laws provide a framework for the accumulation, preservation, and growth of wealth. These are the tenets that, when followed, can result in a prosperous and financially secure existence.

Encapsulated in these laws, the wisdom of Babylon has traveled across ages to reach us with advice and insight into the craft of creating prosperity. We respect the legacy of those ancient bankers and make sure that those who pursue the golden touch of riches continue to benefit from their wisdom as we live by using their principles.

3.2: The Art of Making Money Work for You

Changing one's financial future is possible with the transforming principle of making money work for you. It's the skill of utilizing the money you make to create a tool that brings in more money, creating a vicious cycle of increasing wealth. This idea, which the ancient Babylonians understood well, is the basis of contemporary passive income and financial independence tactics.

What Makes Passive Income What It Is

Being financially independent is ultimately about having a passive income. It is the money received from assets, ventures, or investments in which one does not have a hands-on role. Passive cash comes to you with little continuous work needed to retain it, in contrast to active income, which is directly correlated with the amount of time you work.

Due to their sophisticated knowledge of wealth, the Babylonians were able to generate passive income through a variety of strategies, including interest-bearing loans, property ownership, and company investments. They were able to amass money and experience a degree of financial stability that was not possible with active earning alone because of these revenue streams.

Investing: The Means of Creating Wealth

The act of investing is the distribution of resources, typically monetary, with the goal of making a profit. It is the main way that one can get money to work for them. The Babylonians were astute investors; they invested their gold in businesses that would pay off, such as lending, trading, or farming.

The world of investing prospects has expanded in the modern era. You have a wide range of accessible options to make your money work for you, from the real estate, bond, and stock markets to cryptocurrencies.

Taking Advantage of Compound Interest

The interest computed on the original principal, which includes all of the accumulated interest from earlier periods on a deposit or loan, is known as compound interest. This idea is elegantly expressed in the following formula:

A is equal to $P \left(1 + \frac{r}{n} \right)^{nt}$.

Where:

- After (n) years, the total amount of money accumulated, including interest, is (A).

The principal amount is (P).

The yearly interest rate is denoted as (r) in decimal.

The number of times interest is compounded annually is (n).

- (t) is the number of years that the money is invested or borrowed.

Even though they didn't have this formula, the Babylonians were aware of the idea. As they reinvested their gains, they witnessed an exponential growth in their fortune, leveraging the compound interest effect to their advantage.

Diversification: Dispersing the Wealth-Building Seeds

Spreading investments over different financial instruments, industries, and other categories is a practice known as diversification, which is used to reduce risk. The Babylonians spread out their holdings because they knew that different investments yield positive returns in various circumstances. They should make sure that gains in one region offset losses in another by distributing their wealth around.

Currently, a fundamental component of investment strategy is diversification. It's all about diversifying your holdings so you can withstand various economic downturns and avoid placing all your eggs in one basket.

Understanding Finances: The Secret to Empowerment

Knowledge of finance is the capacity to comprehend and make use of a range of financial skills, including investing, budgeting, and personal financial management. The Babylonians placed high importance on knowledge and made an effort to comprehend the complexities of investing and the building blocks of riches.

Financial literacy in the present period includes a wide spectrum of information, from tax planning to investing techniques, from managing debt to comprehending the stock market. It serves as the cornerstone around which the skill of making money work for you is constructed.

Technology: The New Facilitator

The way we manage our lives has drastically changed due to technology. Finances. Technology offers tools to help automate the process of making money work for you, from investment apps to online banking. The Babylonians kept account of their wealth using abacuses and clay tablets, the instruments of the day. These days, we have access to advanced platforms and tools that, frequently with only a few clicks, may optimize our investments and savings.

For example, robot-advisors can handle a diverse portfolio for you, making adjustments based on your risk tolerance and the state of the market. Investing is becoming less daunting and more accessible thanks to automation, especially for individuals who are new to finance.

Risk Control: Safeguarding Your Assets

Risk management is another aspect of making money work for you. Understanding the dangers associated with various kinds of investment and putting methods in place to reduce those risks. The dangers of investing and trade were known to the Babylonians. They dispersed their fortune among a number of businesses and took safety measures to guard their possessions.

In modern finance, risk management could be diversified across asset classes, including stop-loss orders on stock investments or select investments with a track record of growth and stability.

Leverage: Increasing Your Capability to Invest

Utilizing borrowed funds to invest with the hope that the profits will exceed the interest paid is known as leverage. Leverage raises risk even as it can greatly increase investment rewards. The Babylonians knew that increased risk also carried a higher possibility of return, so they used leverage in the form of loans to improve their trading skills.

Leverage in modern finance might refer to using options or futures contracts, buying stocks on margin, or leveraging a mortgage to invest in real estate. Leverage can be a very effective tool if utilized properly, but it must be handled carefully and with a clear awareness of any potential drawbacks.

Allocating Your Assets: Creating a Portfolio

The strategic distribution of investments among several classifications of resources, including money, stocks, bonds, and real estate, is known as asset allocation. The idea is that since different assets behave differently in various market environments, diversifying will, in the long run, lower risk and increase profits.

Even though the Babylonians did not have access to bonds or the stock market as we know it today, they nonetheless engaged in asset allocation by funding everything from trade missions to agricultural land. They saw that a well-balanced portfolio that could tolerate economic turbulence may lead to ongoing growth.

The Path to Monetary Independence

Financial freedom is the ultimate goal of using money to work for you. When your passive income is greater than your expenses, you are free to live the life you want, free from the constraints of a regular 9–5 job. It's about establishing a life in which you control your schedule and make wise financial decisions with the resources at your disposal.

The Babylonians aspired to a life of self-sufficiency by prudently allocating their money, and they searched for this form of liberty. Although we have more resources and chances than ever before to accomplish this, the fundamental ideas are still the same.

The Value of Time and Patience

Patience is one of the most important things when it comes to making money work for you. The process of accumulating wealth requires time; assets must mature, and compound interest must have time to do its magic. The Babylonians made long-term plans because they understood that time was an ally in the pursuit of wealth.

It cannot be easy to keep this perspective in our fast-paced society, but patience is still a virtue in the financial realm. It all comes down to having a long-term perspective, letting your investments develop, and restraining yourself from taking advantage of every opportunity to profit.

Financial Advisors' Function

The knowledge of their elders and seasoned traders was all that the Babylonians had, but investors nowadays have financial consultants at their disposal. These experts can offer insightful advice that will enable you to manage the complexity of the financial world and choose wisely when it comes to your assets.

An expert financial counselor can help you identify your monetary objectives, assess your level of risk tolerance, and develop an investment plan that supports those goals. They could prove to be a priceless tool in your quest to turn money into something you can use.

The Importance of Lifestyle Decisions

Making wise lifestyle decisions is another aspect of making money work for you. Your financial well-being can be enhanced by living within your means, avoiding needless debt, and giving saving and investing priority over spending.

Although they were accustomed to seeing their wealth on display, the Babylonians also recognized the need for moderation. In the present era, this means avoiding the allure of materialism and concentrating on accumulating riches as opposed to flaunting them.

A Synopsis of The Art of Making Money Work for You

Making money work for you is a complex discipline that includes risk management, investing, saving, using technology, and making wise decisions. It calls for a way of thinking that prioritizes knowledge, perseverance, and thoughtful planning. It all comes down to comprehending the value of diversity, the potential of passive income, and the function of financial counselors.

By becoming an expert in this field, you can put yourself on the road to financial independence, where your money creates more money, and you have complete control over your time. It is a voyage that is still worthwhile and important now, just as it was for the Babylonians thousands of years ago.

In summary, having a sustainable financial ecology that supports your life goals is the key to making money work for you, rather than merely hoarding cash. It's about assuming responsibility for your financial destiny and creating a legacy that is both enduring and transcendent. Money. It is an art that can lead to a life of prosperity and fulfillment if it is practiced wisely and diligently.

3.3: The Value of Sensible Investing

The key to both financial success and wealth building is prudent investment. It's a practice that calls for discipline, foresight, and expertise in addition to skill and knowledge. It is impossible to overestimate the significance of making smart investments since it is how one builds one's legacy and secures one's financial future. Using both the contemporary insights of economic specialists and the ancient wisdom of Babylon, this sub-chapter explores the crucial elements of making prudent investments.

The Meaning of Investing Wisely

A good investment is defined as having a solid grasp of the asset, being in line with one's financial objectives, and taking on a manageable amount of risk relative to the expected return. Every dollar is invested where it has the potential to grow and support one's financial goals since it has been carefully considered and due diligence has been completed.

Famous for their wealth, the Babylonians were careful with their investments. They avoided endeavors that were veiled in uncertainty or that promised unrealistic rewards in favor of possibilities that offered stability and advancement.

The Significance of Research and Carefulness

Sound investment practices are founded on thorough research and due diligence. Getting as much information as you can before investing money in any project is essential. This entails being aware of the state of the market, the investment's history, and the variables that might have an impact on its performance.

Before starting trade, missions or providing finance for expeditions, merchants and dealers in ancient Babylon would obtain information from a variety of sources. Investors may make informed judgments about their investments today because of the abundance of materials available to them, including market analysis and financial reports.

Comprehending Risk and Return

An understanding of the correlation between risk and return is essential to investing. Generally speaking, the risk increases with the possible return. An investor's risk tolerance and financial objectives are taken into account while making wise investments, which creates a balance between the two.

Knowing this balance, the Babylonians would carefully weigh the dangers involved in any venture. To reduce risk, they spread out their holdings and looked for investments that would yield a respectable return without putting them in unnecessary danger.

The Significance of Increasing Variety

The goal of diversification is to lower exposure to any one asset or risk by distributing holdings across a number of asset types. This idea was applied even in antiquity, when the Babylonians used their money to protect themselves by investing in a range of businesses, including trade and agriculture.

To get diversity in contemporary investment, one should maintain a blend of equities, bonds, real estate, commodities, and additional assets. In the long run, this strategy can produce more stable results by reducing market volatility.

The Effect of Time Horizon

An investment's time horizon is the anticipated length of time it will be held before being liquidated. Long-term thinking is often behind wise investment decisions, enabling the investment to weather short-term market swings and benefit from compound interest.

The Babylonians knew that patience pays off when making investments. Even though they would have to wait years for the trees to reach maturity, they would nevertheless plant date groves since they would eventually produce a valuable crop. In a similar vein, contemporary investors are counseled to consider the long term, particularly with regard to retirement savings and other important financial objectives.

Using Financial Advisors

Financial counselors can greatly aid in making smart investing decisions. They provide knowledge, experience, and an unbiased viewpoint that can be quite helpful during the investing process. They can support investors in navigating the often-confusing world of finance and in making well-informed choices that fit their financial goals.

Advisors were sought after in Babylon for their expertise and insight. Qualified financial planners, investment advisors, and wealth managers now provide this service, helping people and families build and safeguard their wealth.

The Importance of Allocating Assets

The process of choosing how to divide one's investments among various asset classes is known as asset allocation. It is a dynamic process that ought to take into account the investor's shifting objectives, risk tolerance, and financial status. A prudent approach to investing entails periodically assessing and modifying one's asset allocation to guarantee that it stays in line with one's goals.

Even though the Babylonians had the complex financial instruments of today, they nevertheless engaged in asset allocation by holding a variety of assets, including products, gold, and land. The abundance of investment options available to modern investors allows them to customize their asset allocation to meet their unique needs.

Compound Interest's Power

For good reason, compound interest is frequently referred to as the eighth wonder of the world. In other words, it's the process via which an investment expands exponentially over time by reinvested interest. Over time, this strong force can increase small deposits to significant amounts.

By lending money at interest and reinvesting their winnings, the Babylonians made use of compound interest. These days, a variety of financial instruments, including stocks, bonds, and retirement accounts, allow investors to tap into this potential.

The Skill of Timing

Although it is typically not advisable to time the market, knowing when to make particular investments can be a sensible component of a well-thought-out investment strategy. This entails understanding life-stage appropriate investing, utilizing dollar-cost averaging, and acknowledging the cyclical nature of markets.

The Babylonians made investments in accordance with these rhythms because they were aware of the passing of time and the cycles of trade. Contemporary investors can apply this idea by keeping an eye out for economic cycles and making timely, well-informed investment selections.

The Moral Aspects

Ethical issues are just as important to wise investing as financial returns. Ecological, social, and governance, or ESG, factors are a component of responsible investing. Because of their sophisticated civilization, the Babylonians were among the first to practice good stewardship, making sure that their investments benefited their city.

Investors now have the chance to fund and invest in businesses that place a high priority on social impact, sustainability, and ethical behavior. This strategy can result in a more satisfying investing experience and matches financial objectives with individual values.

The Significance of Prudent Investing: An Overview

The secret to accumulating and retaining wealth is making wise investments. They necessitate investigation, comprehension of risk and return, diversification, a long-term outlook, and frequent evaluation and modification. They gain from ethical considerations, the power of compound interest, the knowledge of financial counselors, and the smart allocation of assets.

You may guarantee your financial future, leave a lasting legacy, and make a beneficial impact on the world by investing wisely. It is a method that creates a route to success that is both satisfying and long-lasting by fusing the ancient knowledge of Babylon with the contemporary understanding of finance.

4. Chapter 3: The Secret of the Lender

Lenders have played a crucial role in the history of finance. The ability to lend money has always been an essential element in the expansion of economies and empires, from the ancient Babylonian moneylenders to contemporary bankers. However, there is a trick to lending, a little-known fact that makes the difference between bad and successful borrowers. The lender's secret, a treasure trove of knowledge that has been kept hidden for generations, is revealed in this chapter to the astute reader.

The Nature of Lending

Giving money or property to someone else with the expectation that it will be returned—often with interest—is known as lending. It is a long-standing custom that dates back to the dawn of civilization and is based on the knowledge that capital may increase prosperity when used effectively. The art of lending with insight and forethought is just as important as the actual act of lending in becoming a skilled lender.

The Basis of Confidence

Trust is the foundation of lending. Both the borrower and the lender must have faith that the other will treat them properly and that the borrower will return the funds. This mutual trust serves as the foundation for all loans. Before making a loan offer in Babylon, lenders would evaluate a borrower's moral fiber, standing, and capacity for repayment. The idea is still the same; even now, credit ratings and financial documents now serve as a container for this evaluation.

Interest's Power

The lender receives interest as payment for releasing their capital. It is the cost incurred for the right to use someone else's funds. Determining an interest rate that is reasonable, competitive, and appropriate for the risk involved is the key to successful lending. The Babylonians were skilled at this, establishing interest rates that guaranteed they were paid for the risk without subjecting the borrower to excessive burdens.

The Risk Assessment Strategy

evaluation of risk is an essential part of financing. It entails calculating the possibility that the borrower would miss payments on the loan as well as the possible loss the lender could suffer. Here, the key lies in the careful examination of the borrower's financial situation, the loan's objectives, and the overall economic climate. The Babylonians, following the lead of contemporary portfolio theory, would lend to several borrowers in different businesses in order to spread their risk.

The Collateral Art

A thing that the borrower gives the lender as loan security is known as collateral. It serves as the lender's insurance policy, making sure that the lender may recover its investment in the event that the borrower defaults. The key to collateral is accurately assessing it and making sure it has sufficient liquidity to be sold if needed. Lenders in Babylonia frequently demanded collateral in the form of goods or land, which could be readily sold or utilized in the event that the loan was not returned.

The Significance of Records

Written records of the terms and circumstances of the loan serve as the lender's safety net. It's a legally binding contract that requires accountability from both sides. Documentation that is thorough and clear, with no space for misinterpretation, is the key to success. Lenders in Babylonia would write loan agreements with the amount, interest rate, terms of repayment, and collateral on clay tablets.

The Function of Law

The legislative framework that governs lending is provided by legislation. It guarantees that the act of lending benefits society and defends the rights of both lenders and borrowers. Following these rules and laws and conducting business within morally and legally acceptable limitations is the key to effective lending. The regulations of Babylon were severe when it came to lending practices, and laws today are still being developed to safeguard customers and preserve the health of the economy.

The Way Debt Collection Works

The procedure through which a lender obtains money that hasn't been returned in accordance with the loan terms is known as debt collection. The key to successful debt collection is striking a balance between compassion and firmness, realizing that although the lender is entitled to their money, the borrower can actually be having serious problems.

The Responsible Lending Philosophy

The moral component of the lender's trade secret is responsible lending. It is the promise only to give credit when it will most likely help the borrower and not put them in danger of running out of money. Due to their reputation for caution, Babylonian bankers frequently discouraged borrowers from taking out loans that might put them in debt. These days, lending standards and consumer protection regulations are built around responsible lending.

The Synopsis of The Lender's Secret

A patchwork of trust, interest, risk assessment, collateral, paperwork, laws, debt collection, and responsible lending constitutes the lender's secret. The most prosperous lenders throughout history have kept this formula, which has allowed capital to flow and economies to expand, a closely guarded secret.

One can confidently and honorably negotiate the complicated world of money by comprehending and using the lender's secret. It's a secret that once known, opens doors to prosperity in business and prudent asset management.

4.1: Safe Lending Strategy

Since the dawn of civilization, lending has always been a vital component of economic activity, and secure lending practices are just as important now as they were in the ancient Babylonian marketplaces. Safe lending techniques give the borrower the chance to pursue growth while guaranteeing the protection of the lender's capital. This subchapter examines the various aspects of safe lending by referencing both modern financial practices and conventional wisdom.

Knowing the Fundamentals of Safe Lending

The foundation of safe lending is a set of values that safeguard the lender's interests while promoting an equitable and fruitful partnership with the borrower. Thorough risk assessment, suitable interest rates, collateral security, unambiguous terms and conditions, and respect for moral and legal requirements are some of these guiding concepts.

Risk Evaluation: The Cornerstone of Lending

A comprehensive risk assessment is the initial stage of safe financing. This entails assessing the borrower's creditworthiness, stability, and suitability for the intended use of the loan. Lenders have to take into account a number of things, such as credit history, stable income, outstanding obligations, and market conditions.

Lenders in ancient Babylon used a borrower's land holdings, agricultural production, and trade abilities to determine how likely they were to make their payments. In order to make wise selections, lenders nowadays analyze business plans, financial data, and credit scores.

Determining Sufficient and Equitable Interest Rates

Interest rates play a crucial role in the lending process because they allow lenders to recoup their capital-loss risk and opportunity cost. In order to ensure that the borrower can service the debt without experiencing excessive hardship, safe lending requires setting interest rates that are both fair to the borrower and long-term sustainable.

For the purpose of avoiding usury, legislation often governed the fair interest practices of Babylonian lenders, which were well known. In order to set rates that are both competitive and responsible, modern lenders must negotiate a challenging economic environment.

Collateral's Function in Loan Securing

Lenders use collateral as a safety net because it offers a type of security that can be reclaimed in the event that the borrower defaults. Accepting collateral that is sufficiently valued and liquid to support the loan amount is a component of safe lending practices. This could apply to financial assets, equipment, inventory, and real estate.

In Babylon, items or property were frequently used as collateral. Lenders may now request insurance policies or personal guarantees in addition to collateral.

Creating Explicit Terms and Conditions

The legal document that lists the terms and conditions of the loan is called the loan agreement. These conditions must be precise, concise, and understandable to both parties in order to ensure safe lending. This covers the loan amount, interest rate, repayment plan, penalties for default, and any terms or covenants.

Babylonian loan contracts, which included every detail of the debt, were written on clay tablets. Even though modern agreements are increasingly complicated, they still need to be thorough and open.

Respect for Law and Ethical Principles

Safe lending encompasses not only financial stability but also moral and legal morality. Lenders are required to follow legal guidelines and adhere to rules that safeguard borrowers and encourage ethical lending practices.

The Babylonians imposed severe regulations on lending and punished those who behaved unfairly as lenders. Similar to this, modern lenders have to abide by rules like the Equal Credit Opportunity Act and the Truth in Lending Act.

The Value of Record-Keeping and Documentation

Safe lending requires accurate record-keeping and documentation. They offer a record of the transaction, support loan performance monitoring, and act as proof in legal disputes. Lenders are required to keep thorough records of every loan, payment, and correspondence with borrowers.

Records were preserved on sturdy clay tablets in the past. Lenders in the digital age track and manage loans with advanced technologies.

Debt Collection: Striking a Balance Between Firmness and Caring

Lenders need to have a rigorous but sympathetic debt-collecting strategy in place in case of default. Working with debtors to identify solutions—like modifying the loan—before taking legal action is one of the safe lending practices.

Lenders in Babylonia were willing to cooperate with clients, frequently taking partial payments or extending the loan period. Today's lenders have access to a wide range of instruments, such as debt restructuring and collection agency partnerships.

Constant Observation and Evaluation

Continuous portfolio monitoring is necessary for safe lending. Lenders are required to assess the state of the economy as a whole periodically, the borrowers' financial standing, and the performance of their loans. Lenders can detect such problems early and address them with this proactive approach.

Teaching Debtors

Making sure borrowers are aware of their responsibilities and the potential consequences of their loans is a crucial aspect of safe lending. Lenders should give borrowers clear instructions and information so they can comprehend the loan application procedure and their obligations.

A Synopsis of the Safe Lending Strategy

Safe lending is a comprehensive strategy that includes risk assessment, reasonable interest rates, collateral security, unambiguous terms, careful documentation, ethical debt collection, ongoing monitoring, and borrower education. It also complies with regulatory requirements. It's a tactic that helps the borrower reach their financial objectives while safeguarding the lender's capital.

Lenders may create a strong and healthy loan portfolio, support economic expansion, and keep their clients' trust and confidence by upholding safe lending principles. When used wisely and carefully, it is a technique that promotes financial stability and prosperity for all parties involved.

4.2: Evaluation of Risk and Benefit

The wheel of investment revolves around the fine balance between risk and profit. It is an idea that determines whether investing plans are successful or unsuccessful and is firmly embedded in the fabric of financial decision-making. This sub-chapter explores the complex dance of risk and reward assessment, a discipline that, when perfected, can lead to the highest levels of economic success.

The Character of Danger and Gain

In the world of finance, risk and reward are two sides of the same coin. The danger is the potential for sustaining a loss. Or not knowing how an investment will turn out. Conversely, reward refers to the anticipated profit or yield from an investment. The basic reality is that taking on more risk has the potential to generate greater benefits.

Recognizing Different Risk Types

To properly evaluate risk, one must first be aware of its several manifestations. Market risk is the chance that investment returns will change as a result of changes in the market. The chance of a borrower defaulting on a loan is known as credit risk. The possibility that an asset won't be able to be sold soon enough to stop a loss is known as liquidity risk. Technical faults or fraud are examples of internal breakdowns that give rise to operational risk. There are distinct approaches and mitigation strategies needed for each type of risk.

Measuring Danger

Risk quantification is an intricate procedure that incorporates probability theory and statistical analysis. To evaluate risk, investors frequently utilize metrics like standard deviation, beta, value at risk (Var), and conditional value at risk (CVaR). Based on one's risk tolerance, these indicators offer a means to analyze the risk profiles of various assets and make well-informed choices.

Diversification's Function

One important tactic in risk management is diversification. Putting money into a variety of industries, asset types, and regions helps investors lessen the negative effects of a single underperforming investment on their portfolio as a whole. When it comes to risk management, the proverb "Don't put all your eggs in one basket" is accurate.

Investment Horizon and Tolerance for Risk

The ability and willingness of an investor to withstand drops in the value of their investments is known as their risk tolerance. Financial objectives, investment horizon, and individual comfort level with uncertainty are some of the variables that affect it. Since there is more time to recoup from probable losses, a longer investment horizon frequently permits a larger risk tolerance.

The Significance of Reward Evaluation

Even while risk receives a lot of attention, evaluating the potential benefit is just as crucial. This entails evaluating an investment's predicted return to see if it fits with one's financial objectives. Examining past results, possible future development, and the total return on investment are all part of the reward assessment process.

The ratio of Risk to Reward

One technique for comparing the predicted rewards of an investment to the level of risk taken is the risk-reward ratio. When the possible gains outweigh the dangers, the risk-reward ratio is favorable. Investor decisions that are in line with their investment plan and risk tolerance are aided by this ratio.

The Behavioral Facets of Risk Evaluation

Human psychology has a big influence on risk assessment. Poor decision-making can result from behavioral biases such as loss aversion, herd mentality, and overconfidence. By being aware of these biases and using a disciplined investing strategy, one can lessen their impact.

Using Financial Models

Financial models simulate different scenarios and outcomes in order to evaluate risk and reward. The link between risk and expected return can be understood using models like the Black-Scholes model and the Capital Asset Pricing Model (CAPM). Models should, however, be used in conjunction with other assessment tools due to their limitations.

The Effects of Outside Sources

External factors, including political stability, the state of the economy, and changes in regulations, can greatly impact risk and reward. Investors need to keep up with these developments and think about how they might affect their portfolios.

A Synopsis of The Art of Risk and Reward Assessment

A thorough comprehension of financial concepts, a firm grasp of one's financial goals, and an unrelenting dedication to due diligence are necessary for the art of risk and reward assessment. It combines psychological insight, strategic diversification, quantitative analysis, and ongoing learning.

Investors may confidently sail the unpredictable seas of the financial markets by becoming experts at assessing risk and return. When developed, this ability can result in the achievement of long-term prosperity and the fulfillment of financial goals.

4.3: Compound Interest's Power

One of the most potent ideas in finance is frequently praised: compound interest. It's the idea that money expands exponentially over time when interest is reinvested to generate even more income. This section delves into the magic of compound interest and reveals how it may turn even small deposits into substantial wealth.

Comprehending Compound Interest

The interest on a deposit or loan that is computed using the initial principle, as well as the interest that has accrued over time, is known as compound interest. Compound interest allows the growth rate to increase over time since interest is paid on the interest that has already accrued, unlike simple interest, which is computed only on the principal amount.

The compound interest formula is written as follows:

$A = P \left(1 + \frac{r}{n}\right)^{nt}$.

Where:

- is the loan's or investment's future worth, interest included.

The total amount of the initial investment is shown by (P).

The yearly interest rate is denoted as (r) in decimal.

The number of times interest is compounded annually is (n).

- (t) is the loan's or investment's duration. In years.

The Enchantment of Combining

Compounding's power is in its potential to create wealth by allowing earnings to be reinvested. With enough time and a respectable rate of return, a modest amount of money can increase to a significant quantity. This explains why Albert Einstein is said to have referred to compound interest as the most powerful force in the cosmos and why it is commonly cited as the "eighth wonder of the world."

A Historical View on Compound Interest

Compound interest is not a brand-new idea. Compound interest calculations have been understood and applied for ages; historical records show that Babylon and other ancient civilizations used them. Lenders, traders, and merchants understood that if they allowed their money to compound, it may increase dramatically over time.

The Effects of Frequency Compounding

The frequency of compounding can significantly impact an investment's growth. The amount of interest that can be earned on interest increases with the frequency of compounding. For this reason, when all else is equal, accounts with daily or monthly compounding can produce better returns than those with annual compounding.

Time's Function in Compounding

The strength of compound interest is contingent upon time. The consequences of compounding become increasingly noticeable as the time horizon increases. This is the reason it's crucial to begin saving and investing at a young age. Over time, the power of time can produce a remarkable increase in wealth, even with little input.

Compound Interest and Savings for Retirement

Retirement savings is one of the most useful uses of compound interest. Even with modest initial payments, compounding enables people to accumulate a sizeable retirement fund. It serves as the cornerstone for a lot of retirement programs, including IRAs and 401(k)s.

The Impact of Return Rates

Another important component of compound interest's potency is the rate of return. A higher rate of return will cause the principal to rise more quickly. However, since bigger returns typically come with more risk, investors must balance their tolerance for risk against their desire for rapid development.

The Impact of Inflation and Taxes

Taxes and inflation can diminish the advantages of compound interest. Investments that exceed inflation can maintain purchasing power, while tax-advantaged accounts, like Roth IRAs, can lessen the impact of taxes. In order to fully utilize compound interest, it is imperative to comprehend these aspects.

Techniques to Increase Compound Interest

Investors who want to take full advantage of compound interest should begin saving early, make regular investments, and reinvest their returns. In addition, they should look for accounts that offer more frequent compounding and utilize investment vehicles that minimize taxes.

Interest Rate Compounding in Debt Management

In addition to being a tool for growth, compound interest may also be used against people in the form of debt. If not properly handled, credit card balances and loans with compound interest can easily become too much to handle. Compound interest on debt might help people avoid financial hazards if they understand how it works.

An Overview of the Power of Compound Interest

The power of compound interest demonstrates the promise of careful and disciplined investing. Over time, this force has the power to transform small deposits into substantial riches. People can guarantee their financial future and accomplish their financial goals by comprehending and utilizing this power.

5. Chapter 4: The Mentality of the Merchant

Merchants' mindsets are complex fabrics of ambition, strategy, and expertise. Traders and business owners have used this mentality to amass enormous wealth and influence throughout history. This chapter explores the characteristics and behaviors that characterize the successful pursuit of trade, delving into the core mindset of the merchant.

The Entrepreneurial Spirit

The spirit of enterprise—the motivation to produce, trade, and prosper—is at the core of the merchant's way of thinking. This mentality is defined by a steadfast belief in one's potential to succeed, a willingness to take measured risks, and a tireless pursuit of opportunity. The marketplaces of ancient Babylon, where traders exchanged commodities from all across the known globe, were energized by the same energy.

Recognizing the Market

A thorough grasp of the market is a crucial aspect of the merchant's mentality. This includes awareness of supply and demand dynamics, customer behavior, and market competition. Successful merchants' Successful merchants are skilled at spotting holes in the market and tailoring their products to fill those gaps.

Strategic Contemplation

The capacity to organize and carry out actions to achieve long-term success is known as strategic thinking. Merchants with this mentality don't let short-term successes or losses affect them; instead, they look to the future and make decisions to help their businesses succeed in the long run.

The Craft of Bargaining

For traders, negotiating is an art that requires mastery. It requires the deft use of give and take, firmness, and sensitivity to reach compromises that are advantageous to all sides. A merchant's mindset views bargaining as an essential business component that calls for skill, endurance, and psychological awareness.

Prudent Management

Effective money management is the hallmark of financial understanding. This covers financial statement comprehension, investment, and budgeting. Financially astute merchants can make well-informed judgments that optimize earnings and guarantee the long-term viability of their enterprise.

The Value of Interactions

Developing and preserving relationships is essential to the merchant's way of thinking. This covers interactions with partners, suppliers, clients, and rival businesses. Successful merchants know that commerce is not created in a vacuum but rather is the product of innumerable encounters and relationships that need to be fostered over time.

Creativity and Flexibility

The most prosperous retailers share characteristics of adaptability and innovation. They are constantly seeking methods to improve their processes, goods, and services. Additionally, they quickly adjust to market changes brought about by new legal frameworks, customer preferences, or technology breakthroughs.

The Morality of Trade

A key component of the merchant's thinking is ethics. This entails carrying out business equitably, openly, and accountable. Gaining the trust of clients and business associates is crucial for ethical merchants in creating a long-lasting business.

The Influence of Logos

Branding is the process of giving a good or service a distinctive identity. Strong-minded retailers are aware of how important branding is in setting their products apart from those of rivals. A powerful brand has the power to demand premium prices, engender loyalty, and grow into its asset.

The Quest for Greatness

The merchant's mentality is characterized by its desire for excellence. This entails making an effort to provide the greatest goods and services rather than settling for mediocrity. It's an endeavor that calls for meticulous attention to detail, dedication to excellence, and a reluctance to take shortcuts.

The Ability to Overcome Adversities

The capacity to bounce back from obstacles and failures is called resilience. Trade routes are seldom easy, and traders must be ready to overcome challenges with grit and creativity. The merchant has a resilient mindset, seeing obstacles as chances to improve and advance.

An Overview of the Merchant's Mentality

The merchant's mindset is a sophisticated synthesis of aptitude, morality, and experience. Enterprise spirit, strategic thinking, negotiating abilities, financial savvy, relationship development, creativity, flexibility, ethics, branding, excellence, and resilience are all included. Prosperous traders have had this attitude throughout history, from the Babylonian traders to today's corporate executives.

Adopting the mindset of a merchant can help people succeed in their entrepreneurial pursuits and confidently navigate the realm of commerce. When developed, this mindset has the potential to bring prosperity and fulfillment to the business sector.

5.1: The Ethic of Marketing

The psychology of selling involves a sophisticated dance of demands, perceptions, emotions, and wants between the salesperson and the customer. This field explores human psychology's depths to determine what motivates people to make certain kinds of purchases. This section delves into the various facets of selling psychology, offering valuable perspectives on the skill and knowledge of shaping consumer behavior.

Recognizing the Motivation of Purchasers

Understanding buyer motivation lies at the heart of selling psychology. Why does someone select one product over another? The reasons behind them can be as different as the people themselves, ranging from more sophisticated aspirations like prestige and self-actualization to more fundamental wants like protection and security. To successfully influence buyers, sellers need to capitalize on these desires.

The Model AIDA

The AIDA model, a traditional marketing framework, breaks down the customer journey into four steps: attention, interest, desire, and action. Sellers can lead buyers through the sales funnel by grabbing their attention, arousing their curiosity, creating a desire for the goods, and pressuring them to act.

Developing Mutual Understanding and Trust

Building rapport and trust is the cornerstone of effective selling. Customers are more likely to make purchases from reliable and likable sellers. Establishing rapport entails establishing a point of agreement, exhibiting empathy, and genuinely caring about the customer's requirements. The building blocks of trust include dependability, honesty, and keeping your word.

The Power of Feelings

The psychology of marketing heavily relies on emotions. The way that a buyer feels about a product often influences their decision. Sellers Hants can capitalize on emotions by crafting a story around the product that speaks to the buyer's desires or emotional condition.

The Ability to Persuade

The art of persuasion is the capacity to persuade someone to do something. Some persuasive strategies, such as scarcity, authority, reciprocity, and social evidence, may work wonders in sales. Understanding and adhering to these moral guidelines can help sellers better persuade potential customers.

How Cognitive Biases Affect Things

Cognitive biases are regular tendencies to make decisions that deviate from reason. They have a big influence on purchasing decisions. Sellers can effectively manage these prejudices by tailoring their messaging to appeal to typical biases like the bandwagon effect, confirmation bias, and anchoring effect.

Formulating Value Propositions

A value proposition is a brief statement that describes how a product meets a need, offers certain advantages, and persuades the ideal consumer to purchase from you rather than the competition. A thorough grasp of the product's characteristics and benefits and how they meet the consumer's demands is necessary to create attractive value propositions.

The Significance of Effective Communication

Communication must be effective in the sales process. This includes nonverbal clues such as body language, tone of voice, and facial expressions, as well as spoken communication. Sellers must be skilled at communicating their message and hearing the buyer's words.

The Significance of Finishing Methods

The final step in the selling process is closing the deal. It takes poise, self-assurance, and the appropriate selection of closing strategies. The closing strategy—assumptive, urgent, or consultative—must correspond with the buyer's readiness to buy.

Taking Care of Things

Objections are a normal aspect of the sales process. They allow the seller to address concerns and provide more information but do not necessarily indicate disinterest. A possible obstacle might become a selling point if handled gracefully and confidently in response to complaints.

Pricing Psychology

Pricing is a psychological trigger rather than merely a number. How a price is displayed can affect how valuable people think a thing is. Techniques like price anchoring, charm pricing, and bundling can influence a buyer's decision by changing the price perception.

The Morality of Sales

Selling ethically is essential. It entails telling the truth about the goods, abstaining from deception, and ensuring the customer wins the deal. Ethical sellers cultivate long-term relationships with their clients, encouraging referrals and repeat business.

A Synopsis of The Psychology of Selling

Selling psychology is intricate, including a profound comprehension of human behavior, motivation, and decision-making mechanisms. It entails developing relationships, utilizing emotions, becoming an expert persuader, avoiding cognitive biases, creating compelling value propositions, speaking, completing deals, addressing objections, comprehending pricing psychology, and upholding moral principles.

Understanding the psychology of selling can help selling professionals influence consumer decisions, build strong relationships with customers, and increase revenue. In the right hands, this skill set may benefit both the buyer and the seller.

5.2: Adding Worth to Assets

The foundation of wealth creation is value creation. It is the procedure by which companies and individuals generate products or services that are more valuable than the total of their raw materials. This section dives into the complex process of adding value, examining how efficiency, creativity, and strategic thinking support wealth creation.

The Idea of Creating Value

Value creation increases a product or service's perceived worth by the consumer. It's not only about production costs; it's also about the advantages and solutions it offers. Understanding what customers value and exceeding their expectations in delivering it are the cornerstones of producing value.

Recognizing the Needs and Wants of Customers

Developing value begins with a thorough understanding of the consumer's demands and preferences. Trend analysis, consumer input, and market research are needed for this. Businesses can create genuine value by customizing their goods to match their customers' needs by determining what those customers really desire.

The Role of Innovation in Creating Value

Innovation is mostly fueled by value creation. It entails introducing fresh concepts, goods, or procedures beyond accepted norms. Innovation can take many different forms, such as new business models or technical improvements, and it frequently results in higher productivity, improved client experiences, and, eventually, the production of wealth.

Effectiveness and Output

Productivity and efficiency are essential elements in the development of value. They entail maximizing resource utilization, cutting waste, and optimizing procedures. Businesses can directly create value by cutting expenses and raising profitability through increased efficiency.

The Significance of Marketing and Branding

Marketing and branding are effective instruments for creating value. Customers emotionally connected to a powerful brand are more likely to be loyal and willing to pay a premium. Successful marketing communicates the value proposition to the target audience, convincing them of the product's value.

Methodical Pricing

Developing a pricing plan is essential to adding value. Setting a price that accurately captures the product's value to the consumer is more important than merely making ends meet or outbidding competitors on price. Price sensitivity in the target market, the competitive environment, and perceived benefits are all considered when setting a price.

Superiority and Magnificence

Quality can directly determine value. Customers gain value from well-made, dependable goods and services that perform better than expected. Long-term value creation requires a dedication to quality in every facet of the company, from product development to customer service.

The Value of Expandability

A company's scalability is its capacity to expand unhindered by its organizational design or resource availability. Creating scalable value entails implementing procedures and systems that permit expansion without incurring additional expenses. When revenues rise, and costs stay essentially constant, this can result in exponential wealth creation.

Value Creation via Differentiation

Differentiation is the process of setting a product or service apart from rivals. It can be accomplished with distinctive features, excellent craftsmanship, first-rate customer service, or creative design. By establishing the product or service as the go-to option in the market, differentiation adds value.

Using Technology to Create Value

Technology can greatly aid value generation. It may create new markets, improve client experiences, and streamline processes. Companies that use technology well have the potential to generate enormous value for both their clients and themselves.

Long-Term Value and Sustainability

Creating value is about constructing long-term, sustainable prosperity rather than only focusing on short-term gains. This entails considering how company operations affect the economy, society, and the environment. Sustainable business methods guarantee the enterprise's survival and profitability while promoting societal well-being.

The Influence of Connections and Networking

Creating connections and networks can be extremely valuable. Good connections with partners, suppliers, and customers can open new doors and result in greater offers and higher levels of loyalty. Networking can also obtain access to important resources and information that may be used to create riches.

Adding Value to Assets: An Overview

A thorough understanding of customers, creativity, efficiency, smart branding and marketing, suitable pricing, quality, scalability, differentiation, technology, sustainability, and networking are all necessary for creating value for wealth. This is a dynamic and ongoing process. It involves providing goods and services that satisfy customers' needs and exceed their expectations, making money for both the supplier and the client.

Concentrating on creating value can help businesses and people lay a strong foundation for wealth growth. This procedure can result in substantial financial success and a long-lasting legacy if carried out with expertise and vision.

5.3: The Success Code for Merchants

The merchant's code of success is an unwritten set of ideas, tactics, and principles that have aided the financial success of innumerable business owners throughout history. It is timeless and geographically insensitive, encapsulating the fundamental principles of prosperous trade. This subsection aims to clarify these timeless principles, offering prospective business owners a guide to successfully negotiating the murky waters of commerce.

What the Merchant's Code Tenets Are

1. Vision and mission: Every great merchant is driven by a clear vision and a greater mission that goes beyond simply producing money. This vision serves as a source of inspiration for clients and employees and a framework for decision-making.

2. Customer-Centricity: The merchant's code prioritizes the consumer's needs and interests above all else. Since customers ultimately decide whether a firm succeeds, it is imperative that businesses understand and meet their demands.

3. Integrity and Trust: Integrity is the foundation of the merchant's code. It develops a devoted clientele, enhances reputation, and fosters confidence. Successful merchants are recognized for their integrity, dependability, and honesty.

4. Adaptability and Resilience: It's critical to have the capacity to adjust to shifting market conditions and overcome failures. The merchant's code welcomes change and sees obstacles as chances for development and creativity.

5. Knowledge and expertise: Ongoing education and in-depth knowledge in one's industry is critical. The merchant's code values the quest for perfection, skill mastery, and knowledge accumulation.

6. Strategic Planning: Careful preparation and execution lead to success; it does not happen accidentally. Setting strategic objectives, assessing the competitive environment, and making long-term plans are all part of the merchant code.

7. Financial Prudence: One of the merchant code's main tenets is prudent financial management. This covers financial metrics, comprehension, controlling cash flow, investing, and budgeting.

8. Value and Quality: A core tenet is providing clients with high-quality goods and services that are truly valuable. The merchant's code of conduct is to never skimp on quality.

9. Innovation and Creativity: These are essential for staying on the cutting edge. Successful merchants constantly search for fresh concepts, goods, and methods to enhance their operations.

10. Networking and Relationships: Establishing solid bonds with partners, suppliers, and other stakeholders is critical. The merchant's code acknowledges the value of cooperation and networking.

11. Effective leadership and a cohesive team are essential to any successful organization. The merchant code strongly emphasizes developing a culture of teamwork and motivating leadership.

12. Marketing and Branding: To stand out in a crowded market, a company must develop a distinctive brand and promote it successfully. Creating engaging stories that appeal to consumers is part of the merchant code.

13. Persuasion and Salesmanship: The ability to sell is a vital talent. Understanding the psychology of persuasion and effectively expressing the value of one's services are key components of the merchant code.

14. Productivity and Efficiency: Improving productivity and efficiency boosts margins and competitiveness. The merchant's code promotes using technology and streamlining processes.

15. Sustainability and Social Responsibility: A dedication to sustainability and social responsibility is necessary for long-term success. The merchant's code requires them to conduct business in a socially and environmentally responsible way.

The Application of the Merchant's Code

The merchant's code requires continual application of internalized principles to be realized. This includes:

• Establishing a distinct vision and mission for the company.

• Putting the wants and needs of the consumer first when developing new products and providing services.

• Building relationships with clients and partners by operating with unshakable honesty.

• Staying adaptable and strong under pressure from competitors and market turbulence.

• Unwaveringly pursuing knowledge and mastering one's field.

• Using strategic planning to chart a path for expansion and navigate the business environment.

• Prudently handling money, ensuring the business is profitable, and making smart long-term investments.

• Ensuring that each good or service is of the highest caliber and offers genuine value.

• Encouraging innovative ideas and fostering a creative culture inside the company.

• Establishing solid connections and a broad network that can help achieve corporate goals.

• Setting a good example and fostering a culture of excellence and teamwork within the group.

• Create a distinctive brand identity and implement marketing plans that successfully inform the target market about the brand.

• Improving persuasive abilities and sales techniques to clinch agreements and increase clientele.

• Simplifying procedures to increase production and efficiency, which will boost profitability.

• Adopting social responsibility and sustainability, realizing that the health of the community and the environment are entwined with the success of businesses.

An Overview of The Merchant's Code of Success

The merchant's code of success is an enduring manual for individuals aspiring to succeed in business. It supports leadership, networking, marketing, salesmanship, efficiency, sustainability, vision, customer focus, integrity, adaptability, knowledge, strategic planning, financial prudence, quality, and innovation.

By upholding the merchant's code, individuals and companies can attain financial success, a reputation for quality, and a positive influence on their legacy. When followed, this code can result in a successful and rewarding business career.

6. Chapter 5: The Wealth Guardian

One of the main goals of human endeavors has always been wealth in all its manifestations. But just as important as its accumulation is its preservation. The concepts and tactics that guarantee the maintenance and growth of wealth over time are covered in this chapter, "The Guardian of Wealth." It's a story that combines contemporary financial understanding with the knowledge of old guardians.

The Preservation of Wealth Philosophy

The guardian of money follows a different ideology than simple thrift. It is a thorough strategy that includes asset protection, risk management, and planned wealth growth. According to this concept, money should be fiercely acquired and then carefully safeguarded.

Recognizing the Origins of Wealth

Wealth is a dynamic, multidimensional concept rather than a static one. It encompasses both material assets like real estate and cash and immaterial assets like connections, abilities, and expertise. A guardian of wealth must know its complex nature and how factors like inflation, market instability, and obsolescence can undermine it.

Risk Control: The Wealth Shield

Risk management is the wealth-protecting barrier. It entails recognizing possible risks to one's financial security and taking action to lessen them. This includes creating emergency savings accounts, getting insurance, and diversifying investments. Sufficient risk management guarantees that assets are not too vulnerable to possible losses.

Protecting Your Assets: The Wealth Armor

Protecting assets is like wearing armor to keep riches safe. It entails using legal tactics to shield property from creditors, litigation, and other demands. This can involve estate planning, ownership structures, and the usage of trusts. Asset protection ensures that money is safe from outside dangers.

The Wealth Creation Strategy

Strategic expansion is just as important to preserving wealth as defense. Part of this involves investing in assets that appreciate in value over time. It necessitates striking a balance between growth-oriented initiatives that build on principle and conservative methods that safeguard it.

The Significance of Cash

Liquidity is the capacity to swiftly turn assets into cash without suffering a large loss in value. It is a crucial component of wealth preservation since it offers accessibility to money when needed and flexibility. A wealth guardian ensures that some assets are kept liquid to be used for opportunities and commitments.

Estate Planning: The Wealthy's Legacy

Estate planning involves arranging to distribute an estate while a person is still alive. Ensuring that one's preferences transmit wealth and that recipients are cared for is an essential part of wealth preservation. Tax planning, trusts, and wills are all part of estate preparation.

Tax Efficiency: Wealth Optimization

Tax efficiency is the process of organizing one's financial affairs to reduce tax obligations. Since taxes can severely minimize wealth, this is an important guideline. Understanding the tax ramifications of transactions, income, and investments is necessary for tax efficiency.

Financial Advisors' Function

Advisors on finances are allies in the fight to protect wealth. They offer knowledge, direction, and supervision. Financial advisors help guardians of wealth negotiate complicated financial environments, make wise judgments, and keep up with market and legal developments.

Technology's Role in Wealth Management

Technology is now a crucial instrument for managing wealth. It makes information accessible, transactions easier, and investment analysis and monitoring easier. Thanks to technology, wealthy guardians can now handle their assets more precisely and effectively.

Knowledge and Education: The Cornerstone of Preserving Wealth

Knowledge and education are the cornerstones of wealth preservation. It is imperative always to be educated about market trends, investing techniques, and financial principles. A wealthy guardian never stops learning new things to safeguard and increase their possessions.

The Mentality of the Guardian

The guardian has a cautious, anticipatory, and watchful mentality. It is an attitude that is constantly aware of dangers, eager to learn, and forward-thinking. It is a way of thinking that prioritizes sustainability and stability over immediate profits.

An Overview of The Guardian of Wealth

The guardian of wealth is a strategist who wisely and presciently negotiates the difficulties of money as a custodian of financial resources. The guardian's code is composed of the following principles: wealth preservation, risk management, asset protection, strategic growth, liquidity, estate planning, tax efficiency, adviser role, technology utilization, and value of education.

By following this code, people can ensure that their money is increased and protected for future generations. When adhered to, this code results in a lasting legacy, financial security, and peace of mind.

6.1: Safeguarding Your Resources

Safeguarding your assets is the full performance in the vast drama of wealth management. It is the calculated combination of financial planning, risk management, and legal frameworks to protect your hard-earned money from harm. This subsection aims to clarify the intricacies surrounding asset preservation, providing an all-encompassing manual for preserving your financial heritage.

Asset Protection: The Fundamentals

Asset protection is the conscious attempt to prevent one's wealth from being lost, seized, or diminished. It entails a number of financial and legal ploys intended to discourage creditors, lawsuits, or any other organization that might endanger one's assets. Anticipation—seeing possible hazards and acting proactively to reduce them—is the key to asset protection.

Recognizing the Risks to Your Resources

Recognizing the possible dangers your assets may face is the first step in safeguarding them. Lawsuits, divorce settlements, company debts, and even unanticipated creditors may be among them. To make sure that your assets are safe from harm, every threat needs a different approach.

Legal Frameworks for the Protection of Assets

Asset protection can be achieved through a variety of legal frameworks. Trusts, for example, can provide strong protection if properly drafted. Among the tools used to protect assets from possible claims are family limited partnerships, asset protection trusts, and trusts, both domestic and offshore.

First Line of Defense: Insurance

The first line of defense for protecting assets is frequently insurance. Policies like homeowner's insurance, auto insurance, malpractice insurance, and umbrella plans can provide a buffer against claims, ensuring that your assets are not immediately exposed.

Retirement Accounts' Function

Because of national and state regulations, retirement plans such as 401(k)s and IRAs frequently have built-in asset protection features. Making the most of your contributions and being aware of the protections these accounts provide will help you secure your wealth.

Homestead Exemptions

The homestead exemptions provided by certain states shield a portion of a person's home equity from creditors. An extra degree of security can be obtained by being familiar with the homestead laws in your state and organizing the ownership of your residence appropriately.

The Significance of Labeling

An asset's susceptibility can be greatly impacted by its title. Different titling strategies provide various levels of protection, such as community property with the right of survivorship, tenants by the entirety, and joint tenancy. Properly titled assets can avoid being simple pickings in court cases.

Controlling Debt and Reducing Liabilities

Asset protection requires careful attention to debt management and liability exposure reduction. This entails keeping a healthy debt-to-equity ratio, utilizing corporate organizations to reduce personal liability, and separating personal assets from business operations.

Asset Protection and Estate Planning

Estate planning includes safeguarding your assets while you are still alive and arranging for their distribution after your death. Advanced healthcare directives, powers of attorney, and wills are some of the instruments that can guarantee that your assets are handled by your preferences, even in the event of your incapacitation.

Global Asset Defense

International asset protection plans provide an extra degree of security for certain people. Offshore trusts and accounts offer jurisdictional and legal benefits that domestic approaches may not provide. However, they need to be handled cautiously and strictly with tax rules and regulations.

The Application of Secrecy

When it comes to asset protection, anonymity can be quite useful. By owning assets through anonymous corporations or structures, you can protect your riches from prying eyes and public records, making it more difficult for potential plaintiffs to target your wealth.

Continual Evaluations and Updates

Asset protection is not a one-time event that should be ignored. It is vital to regularly examine and update your plans to accommodate changes in legislation, financial situation, and individual circumstances. Maintaining alertness and agility guarantees the continued efficacy of your plans.

The Guardian's Approach to Asset Defense

When it comes to safeguarding your possessions, adopting a guardian's mindset entails being proactive, careful, and strategic. It involves a dedication to comprehending the subtleties of asset protection, consulting an expert, and being ready to take action when required.

Safeguarding Your Resources: An Overview

Anyone hoping to maintain and increase their money must exercise asset protection. This includes a variety of tactics, such as title and debt management, as well as the use of insurance and legal frameworks. By being aware of the risks to your wealth and implementing a thorough asset protection plan, you can ensure that it is safe for future generations.

6.2: Insurance's Place in Preserving Wealth

An indispensable weapon in the toolbox of wealth preservation is insurance. It serves as a safety net against unanticipated events and a guardian for the possessions that people and families have worked so hard to earn. This section examines the function of insurance in safeguarding wealth, examining its several varieties and practical applications.

Knowing Why Insurance Is Needed

Fundamentally, insurance is a tool for transferring risk. In return for a premium, it enables people to transfer the financial weight of possible losses to an insurance firm. This risk transfer is essential to preserving wealth because it offers a safety net that can avert large economic losses.

The Variety of Insurance Products

Numerous products are available in the insurance industry that are intended to safeguard certain facets of wealth. Among them are:

• Life insurance: In the event of the policyholder's passing, it offers beneficiaries financial support.

• Health Insurance: Provides coverage for medical bills, shielding wealth from excessive medical expenses.

• Disability Insurance: Provides replacement of income if a policyholder's disability prevents them from working.

• Property and Casualty Insurance: Guards against loss or damage to tangible things, including houses, vehicles, and personal belongings.

• Liability insurance: Protects against lawsuits from harm or losses inflicted on third parties.

• Long-Term Care Insurance: This type of insurance helps defrays the high costs associated with long-term care services.

• Umbrella Insurance: Provides extra liability protection above and beyond the confines of regular plans.

Life Insurance's Place in Estate Planning

Life insurance is essential in estate planning. It can ensure that heirs are not burdened with debt or taxes, enable the equitable transfer of assets, and give liquidity to an estate. The money received from a life insurance policy can also be used to keep a business operating, support charity donations, and create trusts.

Protection of Wealth and Health

One of the biggest risks to wealth is the cost of healthcare. By paying for hospital stays, operations, and medical bills, health insurance reduces this risk. Selecting a policy that offers sufficient coverage and being aware of the policy's terms and restrictions are essential.

Disability Insurance: Protecting Your Money

A disability-related income loss may severely harm a person's financial stability. Disability insurance provides a percentage of the policyholder's income, enabling them to maintain their level of life and fulfill their financial commitments.

Insurance for Property and Liability: Protecting Tangible Assets

Insurance against property and liability safeguards the material possessions that make up a large amount of a person's wealth. Policies that pay for the cost of upkeep, replacement, or liability related to tangible goods include homeowners' insurance, auto insurance, and personal property insurance.

Insurance for Liability: Preventing Lawsuits

Liability insurance is essential for shielding assets from lawsuits. It can protect the policyholder's assets by paying for court costs, settlements, and judgments in cases involving personal injury lawsuits or claims made against businesses.

Insurance for Long-Term Care: Getting Ready for the Future

Long-term care expenses can swiftly deplete wealth. Long-term care insurance covers home health care, assisted living, and nursing facility care, ensuring that costs don't deplete a person's savings.

Umbrella Insurance: Added Defense

Beyond ordinary plans, umbrella insurance provides an extra layer of liability protection. It provides additional security in the event of significant claims and takes effect when the limits of other policies are reached.

Selecting Appropriate Insurance Plans

Choosing the appropriate insurance policy requires evaluating one's individual goals, risks, and financial status. It necessitates a thorough examination of assets, obligations, and foreseeable demands. Working with a skilled financial counselor or insurance agent can help make educated judgments.

The Insurance Cost-Benefit Analysis

As with any investment, insurance is an investment in security; thus, a cost-benefit analysis is necessary. When comparing premiums, it is important to consider the possible financial consequences of not having coverage. The aim is to find a balance between the required level of protection and cost.

Continual Evaluations and Updates

The requirement for insurance may alter over time due to asset acquisition, life events, or modifications to the legal system. Insurance plans should be reviewed regularly to ensure that wealth is sufficiently secured and coverage meets current demands.

Insurance as a Component of a Wholesome Wealth Preservation Plan

A more comprehensive approach to wealth preservation that incorporates estate planning, investment management, and financial planning should include insurance. It is a component that, when put together properly, completes the image of a stable financial future.

An Overview of Insurance's Function in Preserving Wealth

One essential element of preserving wealth is insurance. It offers defense against a variety of hazards that might jeopardize financial stability. Through reasonable product selection and management, people can protect their wealth against unforeseen catastrophes and guarantee the longevity of their financial legacy.

6.3: Legacy Building and Estate Planning

The last and most important chapters in the history of wealth management are estate planning and legacy development. They are people's way of making sure that their money stays in the family and benefits causes that are important to them and future generations. This section provides a thorough analysis of the methods and factors to be taken into account while creating a legacy that will last.

The Foundations of Estate Planning

Estate planning is making arrangements for an individual's estate administration and distribution both during their lifetime and after death. It entails several financial and legal choices that determine how assets are dispersed, managed, and conserved. Wills, trusts, beneficiary designations, powers of attorney, and healthcare directives are among the essential components of estate planning.

Wills: The Foundation of Eternity

A will is a legal document that specifies the distribution of a person's possessions upon their passing. It serves as a person's legacy blueprint, outlining specific guidelines for the handling of any dependents and the distribution of assets. A well-written will is necessary to avoid disagreements and guarantee that one's desires are carried out.

Trusts: The Channels for Transferring Wealth

Trusts are flexible tools that offer authority over asset distribution. They can specify terms for inheritance, shield assets from creditors, and provide tax advantages. Revocable and irrevocable trusts have distinct functions in estate planning.

Beneficiary Assignments: Allocating Resources

Beneficiary designations are a simple method for transferring assets, including life insurance money, retirement funds, and bank accounts. They take precedence over wills and trusts, so it's critical to maintain them current and in line with an individual's estate strategy.

Authorizations: Transferring Decision-Making Authority

With the use of powers of attorney, people can designate a representative to act on their behalf in the event of an incapacitation. This can apply to judgments made about money, health care, or both. They guarantee that one's affairs are handled by their wishes and are, therefore, an essential part of estate planning.

Healthcare Directives: Maintaining Self-Growth

Healthcare directives offer guidance on medical treatment if a person cannot express their desires. These documents include living wills and medical powers of attorney. They protect individual liberty and help avoid strife within the family in trying times.

Tax Aspects to Take into Account When Estate Planning

Taxes can greatly impact an estate's ability to give money to heirs. The effects of income taxes, inheritance taxes, and estate taxes must all be taken into account while planning an estate. Tax responsibilities can be reduced by employing techniques like gifting, charitable gifts, and the use of specific kinds of trusts.

Giving to Charity: The Philanthropic Facet of Legacy

Giving to charities is a terrific way to support the greater good and ensure that one's legacy reflects one's values. Foundations, charitable trusts, or outright gifts can be used. In addition to offering tax advantages, philanthropy can guarantee that money serves society.

Planning for Business Succession: Sustaining the Enterprise

A crucial component of leaving a lasting legacy for business owners is succession planning. It entails choosing the company's new owner and planning the transition's management. A strong succession plan guarantees the company's continued growth and provides for the needs of its staff members and their families.

The Affective Aspects of Will Drafting

Estate planning includes significant emotional components in addition to financial ones. It encompasses interpersonal connections, family dynamics, and frequently challenging talks. A harmonious estate plan requires navigating these emotional elements with care and open communication.

Professional Advisors' Role

Professional advisers are essential to creating a legacy; these include tax specialists, financial planners, and attorneys specializing in estate planning. They offer the knowledge required to negotiate intricate financial arrangements, legal requirements, and tax rules. Their advice is priceless when drafting an extensive and successful estate plan.

Continual Evaluations and Updates

An estate plan should adapt to changes in a person's life, family, and the law. It should not remain stagnant. Frequent evaluations and revisions guarantee that the estate plan stays applicable and useful in accomplishing the objectives of leaving a legacy.

Creating a Lasting Legacy: Creating an enduring story

The goal of legacy building is to write a tale that lives on after a person's death. It concerns how one's money will affect their neighborhood, family, and the issues they are passionate about. A well-considered approach to legacy creation can leave a long-lasting mark that honors one's goals and principles.

An Overview of Legacy Building and Estate Planning

Estate planning and legacy building are the last acts of financial stewardship and the result of a lifetime of work. They require meticulous preparation, astute judgment, and a thorough grasp of the available economic and legal resources. Through deliberate estate planning and legacy development, people can guarantee that their money will have a significant impact on future generations.

7. Chapter 6: The Road to Plenty

Rather than being a destination, abundance is a journey that takes one through the terrains of action, perseverance and thought. The concepts and behaviors that lead to a life of abundance, where riches are measured in tangible goods and depth of fulfillment and richness of experience, are examined in this chapter, "The Path to Abundance."

The Abundance Philosophy

There is a philosophy of abundance that goes beyond material prosperity. It is an attitude that welcomes the prospect of boundless development, opportunity, and wealth in all spheres of existence. According to this concept, there is enough in the world for everyone to prosper, and we may access this enormous reservoir of potential by the way we think and behave.

Developing an Attitude of Plenty

The cultivation of an abundance mindset is the first step towards achieving abundance. This entails changing from a scarcity mindset—which sees life as a zero-sum game—to a growth-oriented mindset, which sees opportunities everywhere. Having an abundance mindset is all about being thankful, positive, and confident in your abilities to attract and produce money.

Determining Goals

The first step on the path to abundance is to make clear intentions. These are the guiding lights that help you focus your energies and make decisions. Your intentions must be clear, quantifiable, and consistent with your principles and objectives. These are the seeds that give rise to the abundant fruits.

The Influence of Establishing Objectives

The act of identifying your goals and creating quantifiable targets is known as goal setting. As landmarks along the way to abundance, goals offer guidance and inspiration. They should push you to go outside of your comfort zone and be both difficult and attainable.

Formulating a Strategic Plan

A strategic plan is a road map that shows you exactly how to get where you want to go. It outlines the actions you'll take, the materials you'll require, and the schedule you'll follow. A carefully thought-out strategic plan is an essential instrument for negotiating the route to prosperity.

Taking the initiative: The Path to Success

The key to achieving abundance is taking action. Intentions and aspirations become realities when they are consistently and deliberately pursued. It takes discipline, dedication, and a strong will to work hard and overcome obstacles to take action.

The Significance of Individual Growth

Personal growth is a continuous process of self-improvement that improves one's capacity to generate abundance. It entails increasing one's emotional intelligence, knowledge, and aptitude. Personal development aims to become the best version of oneself and accomplish great things.

Wealth Education and Financial Literacy

Monetary plenty is predicated on financial literacy. It entails comprehending the fundamentals of investing, wealth building, and money management. With the help of wealth education, you can increase your money prudently and make well-informed financial decisions.

Purchasing Wealth-Generating Assets

One essential component of creating wealth is investing. It entails assigning funds to assets with the potential to produce revenue or increase in value. Whether investing in real estate, stocks, companies, or other assets, the secret is to make informed decisions and handle your money well.

Generating Several Revenue Sources

Having several sources of income helps hasten the path to wealth and provides financial stability. These may consist of investments, side ventures, passive income, and more. By spreading out your revenue, you can ensure that you are not dependent on any one source and that your wealth will keep increasing.

The Significance of Physical and Mental Welfare

Real abundance includes health and happiness in addition to material prosperity. Maintaining your physical, mental, and emotional well-being is crucial to fully appreciate the riches you earn. A healthy lifestyle gives you the vitality and energy to reach your objectives.

Developing Connections and Networking

Networking and building relationships are essential to achieving abundance. They provide support, let you know about fresh opportunities, and add deep connections to your life. Developing a solid network can help you advance and improve your trip.

Returning the Favor: The Cycle of Plenty

One of the most important lessons on the road to prosperity is giving back. It reaffirms the notion that we multiply our wealth through sharing it. Engaging in philanthropic giving, mentoring, and community service are means to add to the abundant cycle and make a good influence that goes beyond oneself.

The Way to Plenty: An Overview

A good outlook, clear intentions, goal-setting, strategic planning, action, personal growth, financial literacy, prudent investing, various income streams, relationships, health, and giving back are all important components of the holistic route to wealth. Anybody can follow this route, regardless of where they are in life.

Adopting the concepts discussed in this chapter can help you start down your path to abundance and build a prosperous, happy, and fulfilled life. Although this road demands commitment and work, the benefits are enormous and go well beyond monetary achievement.

7.1: The Path to Personal Development

The pursuit of personal development and self-actualization through self-improvement is a lifetime odyssey. It's a road paved with hardships and victories, reflection and learning, self-control and change. This subsection clarifies self-improvement's complexities and guides how people might start this life-changing process.

Recognizing Your Improvement

Self-improvement is deliberately making decisions that result in a more contented and satisfied existence. It involves determining areas for improvement, establishing objectives to reach those goals, and acting consciously to achieve them. Every person's path toward self-improvement is distinct and reflects their own goals, principles, and worldview.

The Significance of Introspection

Self-awareness is the cornerstone of self-improvement. It entails being aware of your emotional reactions, values, and beliefs, as well as your strengths and shortcomings. Self-awareness helps you develop meaningful goals and see areas that require adjustment.

Establishing Personal Objectives

Establishing goals is an essential first step in improving oneself. Objectives give guidance and meaning, acting as standards for advancement. SMART (specific, measurable, attainable, relevant, and time-bound) goals are effective. They ought to push you to reach beyond your present comfort zone while being reachable.

Creating a Growth Mentality

A growth mindset is the idea that skills and intelligence can be developed through commitment and effort. It opposes a fixed mindset, which holds that aptitudes and skills are unchanging characteristics. A growth mindset is necessary for self-improvement since it promotes resilience, learning from mistakes, and ongoing improvement.

The Significance of Habits in Enhancing Oneself

Habits are the foundation of self-improvement. These are modest, everyday deeds that, when added together, make a big difference. Creating healthy routines like regular exercise, mindful eating, or lifelong learning can make a big difference in your quest for personal development.

Accepting Lifelong Education

Seeking information and skills continuously is known as lifelong learning. It is essential to developing oneself since it keeps you sharp, mentally, and flexible. Learning throughout your life broadens your horizons and improves your quality of life, whether it is through formal schooling, reading, or new experiences.

The Influence of Journaling and Reflection

Journaling and introspection are two techniques that help with self-improvement. They let you reflect on the past, draw lessons from it, and make plans for the future. By keeping a journal, you can keep track of your progress and understand your personal development.

Overcoming Difficulties and Failures

The road to self-improvement is not devoid of roadblocks and disappointments. It takes adaptability, resilience, and a positive outlook to overcome these obstacles. Successful self-improvement is characterized by viewing setbacks as learning opportunities rather than failures.

Requesting Mentorship and Input

Mentorship and constructive criticism are helpful when trying to improve oneself. Mentors can provide direction, encouragement, and support, while constructive criticism offers an outsider's viewpoint on one's development. Both can hasten one's progress and support one as one negotiates the challenges of personal growth.

The Value of Good Mental and Physical Health

Enhancing one's physical and mental well-being is essential for personal growth. Maintaining the energy and focus required for personal development depends on taking good care of your body through exercise, proper diet, and rest, as well as your mental health through stress reduction, mindfulness training, and counseling.

Keeping Ambition and Contentment in Check

Although self-improvement is fueled by ambition, contentment must be balanced with ambition. A rewarding road of self-improvement requires appreciating your accomplishments, living in the present, and retaining gratitude.

The Effects of Improvement on Oneself on Others

Enhancing oneself not only helps you, but it also makes people around you happy. As you mature, you inspire others, evolve into a role model, and make a positive impact on society and your community.

The Path of Self-Improvement: An Overview

Self-improvement is a lifetime task that includes developing positive habits, a growth mindset, self-awareness, goal-setting, reflection, overcoming setbacks, getting feedback, maintaining one's physical and mental well-being, and striking a balance between ambition and satisfaction. It's a voyage that makes you stronger, broadens your horizons, and positively affects people around you.

Committing to better yourself sets you on a course for ongoing development that results in a richer and more satisfying life. Although this road demands commitment and work, the benefits are enormous and go well beyond individual achievement.

7.2: Developing Yourself to Create Wealth

Many people believe that accumulating wealth involves making numerous financial plans and investing choices along the way. Ultimately, nevertheless, the goal of personal growth is intrinsically related to the process of accumulating wealth. This sub-chapter explores the intricate relationship between financial prosperity and personal development, showing how developing one's character and mind can result in the accrual of material wealth.

The Relationship Between Self-Growth and Wealth

Wealth is more than just a collection of possessions; it is a reflection of one's capacity and personal development. By improving one's knowledge, abilities, and mindset, personal growth accelerates the process of creating wealth. The lens of personal development is used to recognize, seize, and cultivate chances for riches.

Developing an Attitude of Wealth Consciousness

The formation of a wealth-conscious attitude is the cornerstone of accumulating money via personal growth. This way of thinking is defined by a steadfast faith in plenty, an emphasis on possibilities rather than challenges, and the assurance to make wise financial decisions. It sees wealth as a result of creating value rather than as a limited resource.

Financial Education's Function

One of the most important aspects of human growth is financial education. It entails comprehending the fundamentals of investing, money management, and economic trends. A person with a good education may spot profitable investments, make well-informed decisions, and stay away from traps that can result in loss of money.

Creating High-Profit Capabilities

Certain abilities are in high demand in the current economy. Gaining expertise in high-paying fields like sales, digital marketing, or coding can greatly increase one's earning potential. Developing oneself in these areas can lead to prospects for consultancy work, entrepreneurship, and higher pay.

Networking's Power

Networking can help one build money and advance one's personal development. It entails making connections with others who can offer support, collaboration, and mentoring. A strong network can facilitate access to commercial possibilities, job growth, and wealth-building techniques.

Accepting Lifelong Education

The ongoing pursuit of knowledge and skill is known as lifelong learning. It refers to keeping up with market dynamics, emerging technology, and financial trends in the context of wealth building. Individuals who pursue lifelong learning are more advantageous in seizing new possibilities and navigating the dynamic economic environment.

Productivity's Effect on Wealth

The effective use of time and resources to get desired results is known as productivity. It entails forming routines and procedures that optimize productivity and efficacy in personal development. Enhanced productivity can result in wealth accumulation through professional development and entrepreneurial success.

Allocating Resources for Individual Well-being

Investing in one's health is crucial and directly affects accumulating wealth. People in good health can work harder, think more clearly, and produce more. A good diet, exercise, and stress management can help achieve a long, active career and avoid expensive medical costs.

Why Emotional Intelligence Is Important

Emotional intelligence is the capacity to comprehend and regulate one's own emotions as well as those of others. It is an important tool for personal growth because it improves decision-making, leadership, and communication abilities. Several abilities are necessary to create and preserve riches.

Getting Rid of Limiting Thoughts

Negative presumptions, known as limiting beliefs, might impede one's ability to flourish financially and personally. Overcoming these misconceptions is a critical first step in personal development. It entails overcoming negative mental habits, cultivating a positive view of oneself, and accepting the notion that achieving financial success is possible.

The Craft of Visualization and Goal-Setting

Techniques like goal-setting and visualization can help close the gap between generating riches and advancing one's development. By establishing specific financial goals and envisioning achievement, a person can map out a strategy for building wealth and ensuring that their behaviors are consistent with their financial goals.

The Morality of Wealth

When chasing wealth, ethical issues must come first. Developing a feeling of accountability, justice, and integrity is a part of personal development. Wealth that is based on moral principles is more likely to last and benefit society.

Creating Wealth via Self-Development: An Overview

A wealth-conscious attitude, financial knowledge, high-income skills, networking, lifelong learning, productivity, health, emotional intelligence, overcoming limiting beliefs, goal-setting, visualization, and ethics are all part of the holistic approach to building wealth via personal development. It's a path that leads to a richer, more satisfying life in addition to financial success.

By investing in their personal growth, people may reach their full potential, add value, and clear the path to financial plenty. This route calls for perseverance, discipline, and a dedication to lifelong learning.

7.3: Wealth Is Not Just Financial

It is simple to lose sight of life's intangible treasures in the chase of money and become entangled in the measurable. This sub-chapter, "The Riches Beyond Money," explores riches invested in a person's soul and spirit rather than money that can be put in a bank. It's a story that aims to redefine riches to encompass all the various gems that make life more meaningful.

Redefining Affluence

Money, assets, and tangible belongings are frequently used to measure wealth. True wealth, however, goes well beyond these measurements. It includes the quality of our relationships, the depth and breadth of our experiences, the scope of our knowledge, and our impact on the world. Including these components in the definition of wealth offers a more comprehensive understanding of what it means to lead a wealthy life.

The Value of Connections

One of the most important sources of non-monetary wealth is human ties. Solid bonds with friends, family, and the community give one support, affection, and a feeling of acceptance. They are the thread that runs through our life's tapestry, bringing warmth and color to our being.

The Benefits of Experience

The currency of a life well lived is experience. They mold our personalities, influence our viewpoints, and produce the treasured memories we hold dear. The wealth of knowledge is a treasure that money cannot purchase, whether by exploring new locations, taking on new experiences, or just enjoying the little things in life.

The Importance of Wisdom and Knowledge

Wisdom and knowledge are priceless gifts that enhance life's richness. Learning new things, developing new abilities, and trying to understand the world are worthwhile undertakings that lead to enlightenment and personal development.

The Wealth of Health and Welfare

A life of plenty is predicated on having good health and well-being. While mental and emotional well-being enables us to face life's obstacles with grace and perseverance, physical health allows us to participate fully in the world. Putting money into one's health is an investment in one's life quality.

The Plenty of Time

Since time is a limited resource, the way we choose to use it reveals the values and priorities we hold dear. Engaging in pursuits that make you happy, fulfilled, and meaningful is a wise use of time. It is the most valuable asset of a life full of accomplishments and experiences.

The Good Fortune of Originality and Personal Expression

Self-expression and creativity are great sources of wealth. They allow us to express our viewpoints, contribute to the world's beauty, and make a lasting impression. The act of creation, in all its manifestations, demonstrates the richness of the human soul.

The Value of Volunteering and Giving

Serving others and improving the lives of others are two effective methods to improve our own. Generosity and selflessness spread happiness like a virus, giving people a feeling of direction and community. Giving is a sign of the abundance that arises from having an open heart.

The Impact and Contribution Legacy

We measure a different kind of wealth based on our contributions to society and our impact on the planet. These are the traces of our heritage, the marks we make on humanity's history. Making an effort to improve things is a noble endeavor that benefits both the world and ourselves.

The Abundance of Contentment and Inner Peace

The deepest kinds of wealth are inner contentment and calm. They result from living a life that is consistent with our beliefs, appreciating the present moment, and practicing thankfulness for what we have. The demands of the material world are banished from this inner prosperity, which serves as a haven.

Freedom and Autonomy's Riches

Autonomy and freedom are priceless gifts that let us live life as we see fit. They allow us to follow our passions, make our own decisions, and be ourselves. The wealth of self-determination comes with the privilege of choosing our path.

The Abundance of Spirituality and Religion

Spirituality and faith are huge sources of wealth for a lot of people. They offer a foundation for comprehending the world, consolation during difficult times, and a group of others who share similar beliefs. Via institutionalized religion or individual spiritual practice, these qualities provide life context and significance.

The Wealthy Beyond Cash: An Overview

The riches that transcend money are the things in life that bring true happiness and contentment. Relationships, experiences, wisdom, health, time, creativity, generosity, influence, freedom, inner peace, and spirituality are a few of them. These are the enduring assets, the wealth that matters most in the scheme of things.

We can live affluent lives by appreciating and acknowledging the treasures beyond money. This viewpoint encourages us to pursue richness in our hearts, thoughts, and souls and in our bank accounts.

8. Conclusion: Babylon's Richest Man of Today

As we close our investigation into money and prosperity, we come to a suitable conclusion: the Richest Man in Babylon of today. This title is not given to a single person; rather, it is a composite of ideas, methods, and ways of thinking that have endured through the ages and been modified to fit the complexity of the modern world.

The Development of Wealth

According to the traditional parables, the Richest Man in Babylon accumulated riches by using knowledge of the laws of gold, wisdom, and self-control. The modern-day equivalent of this person would be someone who integrates global knowledge, cutting-edge technology, and time-tested financial concepts. This person knows that wealth is dynamic and changes with the economy, society, and technology.

The combination of the Ancient and the Modern

The Richest Man in Babylonia of today is a harmonious fusion of cutting-edge invention with age-old knowledge. He applies the fundamental principles of prudent saving, intelligent investing, and seeking advice, but he also takes advantage of the digital age's resources and opportunities, such as global markets, fintech, and cryptocurrencies.

The Abundance Mindset

The abundance attitude is essential to the success of the modern-day Richest Man in Babylon. This way of thinking goes beyond the idea of scarcity and instead concentrates on adding value, taking advantage of chances, and developing a giving mindset. It views wealth as a resource that may grow and benefit many people rather than a zero-sum game.

Education and Financial Literacy

Financial literacy is more important than ever in today's market. Our era's version of the Richest Man in Babylon is knowledgeable about economic indicators, investing techniques, and money matters. He keeps up with the most recent developments in finance and recognizes the value of lifelong learning.

Diversification and an International View

Even though diversification today includes a worldwide portfolio, it is still a crucial wealth preservation tactic. By spreading his investments across asset classes, sectors, and regions, the modern-day Richest Man in Babylon reduces risk and takes advantage of emerging markets' growth potential.

Wealth Management and Technology

A key component of wealth management is technology. Today's Richest Man in Babylon uses technology—from blockchain ledgers to robot-advisors—to improve decision-making, efficiency, and security in his financial dealings.

Ethical Investing and Sustainability

In addition to his own money, the modern Richest Man in Babylon is also concerned with his investments' long-term viability and moral ramifications. He participates in impact and socially responsible investing and back programs that advance social justice and environmental conservation.

Wealth and Health and Well-Being

The Richest Man in Babylon today invests in his physical and mental well-being because he understands that true prosperity encompasses health and happiness. He knows that appreciating and managing his fortune depends on having a healthy body and mind.

The Significance of Mentoring and Legacy

The ideology of the contemporary Richest Man in Babylon is fundamentally based on mentoring and the desire to leave a lasting legacy. He aims to impart his expertise and experience to the following generation to ensure that his riches have a beneficial and long-lasting effect.

Flexibility and Sturdiness

Resilience and flexibility are critical traits in a constantly changing world. Today's Richest Man in Babylon is nimble and capable of confidently navigating technological advancements, market upheavals, and economic cycles with strategic vision.

The Wealthy Beyond Cash

Ultimately, the Richest Man in Babylon of today understands that there are riches outside of money, such as relationships, experiences, wisdom, and the satisfaction of leading a meaningful life. He assesses his riches based on the quality of his life's experience rather than just his material possessions.

In summary

The Richest Man in Babylon of today is a lighthouse for the future rather than a remnant from the past. Though he is firmly grounded in the present and has an eye on the future, he exemplifies the values that have historically led to prosperity. His narrative demonstrates a sense of harmony between custom and innovation, wealth and well-being, and self-interest and the greater good.

As we conclude this research, let's apply the lessons learned from the Richest Man in Babylon to our own lives and times. May everyone follow the road to prosperity with discernment, moral rectitude, and a timeless vision.

Putting together a thorough guide on resources and tools for financial growth is a terrific approach to arm people with the information they need to make better financial decisions. An interesting article covering a variety of financial tools and resource topics may be found below:

9. Appendix: Financial Growth Instruments and Resources

Overview

Achieving financial success is a journey that calls for thoughtful preparation, persistent work, and the appropriate equipment. Having the correct resources at your disposal may make a big difference, regardless of your experience level or inexperience. This appendix provides a carefully selected list of tools and resources to help you prosper financially.

Cost tracking and budgeting

Budgeting is the foundation of personal finance. It is critical to prepare for both short—and long-term needs and to be aware of where your money is going each month.

Instruments:

• Mint: This app facilitates budgeting, spending tracking, and increased savings.

• You Need a Budget (YNAB): YNAB helps you be more deliberate with your spending by putting a purpose on every dollar.

• Pocket Guard: This tool makes budgeting easier by displaying your disposable money after expenses, savings targets, and bills have been paid.

Platforms for Investing

One effective strategy for gradually increasing money is investing. Various platforms are available to accommodate diverse investment objectives and approaches.

Instruments:

• Robinhood: Provides commission-free stock and cryptocurrency trading.

• Acorns: Uses the extra change to invest your purchases after rounding them to the next dollar.

• Vanguard: renowned for offering long-term investors low-cost index funds and ETFs.

Debt Control

For financial progress, debt management and repayment are essential. You can monitor and plan your debt repayment with the aid of these resources.

Instruments:

One useful tool to help you plan the quickest route out of debt is Unbury. Me, a loan calculator.

• Debt Payoff Planner: Offers a detailed strategy for paying off debt by avalanche or snowball methods.

Tracking Credit Scores

One of the most important aspects of your financial wellness is your credit score. Keeping an eye on your credit can help you get better-rate loans.

Instruments:

• Credit Karma: Provides free credit score monitoring and updates.

• Experian: Offers credit reports, ratings, and fraud and identity theft monitoring.

Retirement Strategy

Retirement planning is a long-term financial objective. These resources can help you monitor your progress and estimate your retirement needs.

Instruments:

• Personal Capital: Provides a free financial dashboard for monitoring your finances along with wealth management services.

The Bloomberg Retirement Calculator can help you determine how much you need to save for retirement, using your current age, salary, and savings rate as a guide.

Setting Up Your Taxes

While taxes might be complicated, with the correct tools, you can make the process easier and make sure you're taking advantage of all available credits and deductions.

Tools: • TurboTax: Use its intuitive interface to guide you through tax preparation.

• H&R Block: Provides in-person tax preparation services as well as do-it-yourself tax software.

Instruction and Acquiring Knowledge

Maintaining current knowledge of best practices and financial trends requires ongoing education.

Resources: • Investopedia: Offers a plethora of knowledge about financial concepts and investments.

• Khan Academy: Provides free classes in economics and personal finance.

- Coursera: Provides university-level courses on investing and finance.

Community and Networking

Getting involved in a group of people who share your values might help you gain support and knowledge on money-growth tactics.

Resources: • Reddit forum r/personal finance: This is a place for conversations about personal finance.

- Bogle heads: An online community focused on Vanguard founder John Bogle's investment philosophies.

Efficiency and Automation

You may save time and prevent missing payments and investment possibilities by automating your finances.

Instruments:

- If This Then That (IFTTT): This feature enables you to programmatically trigger various online services to do things like save money when you reach your fitness objectives.

- Zapier: This tool connects your preferred apps and streamlines processes that can be applied to financial tasks.

In summary

The information and techniques in this appendix are merely the beginning of your journey toward financial growth. By utilizing these tools, you can make wiser decisions, take charge of your finances, and put yourself on the road to financial success. Recall that consistency, education, and a readiness to adjust to new tools and techniques as they become available are essential for financial success.

Wealth's Ancient Secrets: Unveiling The Richest Man in Babylon

www.ingramcontent.com/pod-product-compliance
Lightning Source LLC
Chambersburg PA
CBHW071200240526
45470CB00017B/618